20 THINGS WE'D TELL OUR TWENTYSOMETHING SELVES

PETER AND KELLI WORRALL

MOODY PUBLISHERS

CHICAGO

Published in association with the literary agency of Wolgemuth & Associates.

Edited by Pam Pugh
Interior design: Ragont Design
Cover design: Thinkpen Design
Cover photo copyright © by 23pictures/Shutterstock (211860766). All rights reserved.
Author photo: Chris Popio

Many names have been changed to protect the privacy of friends and family.

Library of Congress Cataloging-in-Publication Data

Worrall, Peter.
20 things we'd tell our twentysomething selves / Peter and Kelli Worrall.
  pages cm
Includes bibliographical references.
ISBN 978-0-8024-1334-5
  1. Young adults--Conduct of life. 2. Young adults--Religious life. I. Title. II. Title:
Twenty things we'd tell our twentysomething selves.
BV4529.2.W675 2015
248.8'4--dc23

2015014753

We hope you enjoy this book from Moody Publishers. Our goal is to provide high-quality, thought-provoking books and products that connect truth to your real needs and challenges. For more information on other books and products written and produced from a biblical perspective, go to www.moodypublishers.com or write to:

Moody Publishers
820 N. LaSalle Boulevard
Chicago, IL 60610

1 3 5 7 9 10 8 6 4 2

Printed in the United States of America

Praise for
20 Things We'd Tell Our Twentysomething Selves

20 Things We'd Tell Our Twentysomething Selves is packed full of wisdom that is eye-opening, practical, and inspirational. From the all-important first step—check your worldview—to the final piece of encouragement, prepare to be challenged and equipped! Each chapter is a wonderful mix of relevant research, personal stories, and biblical truth. Peter and Kelli Worrall write with authenticity about their own journey toward discovering and implementing these 20 Things. And they serve as compassionate and engaging mentors for anyone hoping to make the most of this significant decade of life. This is now one of the top books I will recommend for twentysomethings.

—SEAN MCDOWELL, PhD, professor at Biola University, popular speaker, and the author of more than fifteen books

I love this book. It's everything I wish I had when I was approaching my twenties and so needed for young adults today.

—JEFF GOINS, bestselling author of *The Art of Work*

Imagine the pressure of writing an endorsement for your college English professor! I am one of the blessed twentysomethings mentioned in this book who was regularly invited out to Peter and Kelli's home during my college years for tea, respite from the stresses that come along with being a college student, and life advice. The biblical, practical wisdom that the Worralls faithfully and patiently imparted to me over those four foundational years was greatly used by God to alter the course of my life, and that same wisdom is now contained in the pages of this book, for you. So go make yourself a good cup of British tea, and settle in for twenty life-lessons that will aid, assist, sharpen, and steer you in your journey toward becoming a faithful disciple of Jesus.

—LINDSAY MCCAUL, singer and songwriter

Peter and Kelli were the featured speakers at our recent college ministry retreat where they taught through the topics now captured in this book. The *20 Things* immediately struck a chord with our group of college-age young people. The Worralls speak and write from personal life experience, which makes their insights authentic and relatable. The young adults I work with are hungry to address the very topics covered by *20 Things*, and I'm excited to make this book a key recommendation in our ministry. Whether you're a twentysomething looking to grow or a ministry leader hoping to impact the next generation, Peter and Kelli's book is a fantastic resource.

—ERIC NAUS, pastor for university students, The Moody Church, Chicago

Kelli and Peter's experiences are relatable, their advice is grace-filled and gentle, and their thoughtful discussion questions encourage vulnerability and community. I wish I'd known them in my twenties!

—ADDIE ZIERMAN, author of *When We Were on Fire: A Memoir of Consuming Faith, Tangled Love, and Starting Over*

A beautiful book. Peter and Kelli Worrall write words so meaningful and helpful, you feel as if they wrote the entire thing just for you. It makes me want to go through my twenties all over again, just for the pleasure of doing so with their excellent advice.

—TYLER HUCKABEE, writer and former managing editor of *RELEVANT Magazine*

I have had the privilege of working with twentysomethings for over a decade as both their professor and their pastor, and I've come to realize that being in your twenties today is very different than it was two decades ago. It is also a much more difficult terrain to hike through. In *20 Things* Peter and Kelli Worrall provide invaluable and much-needed godly wisdom for young people navigating the transition of emerging adulthood: that state of being no longer children, but not quite adults in a traditional sense. Peter's and Kelli's own experiences traversing the twenties ridge trail, along with their combined years of ministry with twentysomethings, gives them a unique empathy for the challenges often misunderstood by church leaders and a vision for a path to flourishing adulthood.

—JOEL WILLITTS, professor of biblical and theological studies, North Park University, Chicago

For our students—
past, present, and future.

contents

WHY THIS BOOK?

No matter who you are, where you live, or what you're doing, if you're in your twenties you are undoubtedly experiencing a decade of some transition—whether it be big or small.

You may be making career decisions, relationship decisions, geographic decisions, or education decisions. You may be living with family, you may be launching out on your own in the big city, or you may be packing your bags to move to some remote island in the South Pacific to serve with the Peace Corps.

You may have landed an entry-level position at your dream company, you may be making lattes at a trendy espresso bar, or you may be pounding the proverbial pavement with a stack of resumes, wondering when some door—any door—is going to swing open for you. You may be married, you may already have kids, you may be wondering whether your current significant other is "the one," you may be tweaking your account with an online dating service, or you may be enjoying the single life. Regardless, for most of you in your twenties, your time of formal education and dependence and externally imposed structure is coming to an end, and suddenly "adult life"—whatever that means—must begin.

In generations gone by, this was typically a simpler shift. Children more frequently followed in the footsteps of their parents. Options were more limited, and expectations were often imposed. If a mother was a seamstress, she likely taught her daughter the craft. If a father was a lawyer, his firm often added "& Son" to the shingle after his offspring passed the bar. For many twentysomethings in the past, setting a course for life was straightforward and even predetermined.

Times, of course, have changed. Today's twentysomethings face a future of innumerable opportunities. You can travel to exotic destinations. You can continue your education in many different and increasingly convenient ways. You can find jobs all around the globe. You can "meet" people from all walks of life, and if you don't want to, you don't even have to leave the comfort of your kitchen table.

Some of you may get excited about all of the possibilities to experiment and explore.

But many of you also look ahead with some measure of fear.

A "QUARTERLIFE CRISIS"?

Alexandra Robbins and Abby Wilner coined the term "Quarterlife Crisis" to describe this period of life. They interviewed dozens of twentysomethings and found that an overwhelming majority of them were experiencing some sense of confusion and helplessness, disappointment, and even panic. Many feel the pressure that "the choices they make during this period will influence their thirties, forties, fifties, and on, in an irreparable domino effect."[1]

As professors at a Bible college, Kelli and I are privy to both the anticipation and the anxiety of many twentysomethings. Every week students and recent grads come to our offices and our home and confess their concerns. They wrestle aloud with issues of direction and identity. But most of these conversations could be boiled down to one central question: *How do we make wise choices?*

SINGLE FOCUS

Sadly, when it comes down to it, too many of us do not even make choices at all. Instead we let the waves of life toss us and the current of the culture carry us along. However, as Alexander Maclaren powerfully points out in his sermon on King Solomon, not making a strong choice *is* a choice in itself—a choice to drift. "There is more evil than good in the world," Maclaren writes, "and if a lad takes his colour from his surroundings, the chances are terribly against his coming to anything high, noble, or pure. This world is no place for a man who cannot say 'No.' If we are like the weeds in a stream, and let it decide which way we shall point, we shall be sure to point downwards. It would do much to secure the choice of the Good, if there were a clear recognition by all young persons of the fact that they have the choice to make, and are really making it unconsciously."[2]

At the start of his reign, when he was a young twentysomething, King Solomon had a choice to make. God came to him in a dream and said, "Ask what I shall give you" (1 Kings 3:5). Would Solomon set his heart on God, or on some other objective? He set it, mostly, after God. He asked God for wisdom, an understanding heart to judge between good and evil. But wisdom was really a tool for him to use in seeking his primary goal—to know the mind of God.

What have you set your heart on? Is God a tool in your toolbox that enables you to achieve your goal? Or is God Himself the goal?

In Jesus' first talk to His newly minted disciples on a Galilean hillside, He called them to such a commitment. The young men and women on that hill had committed to a Person when they agreed to follow Jesus, but they weren't really clear who He was or where He was going to lead them. It would take them a lifetime to find out. They worried about how they would pay their bills, what they might eat for dinner, or what clothes they could afford to buy. But in the Sermon on the Mount, Jesus told them that life was more than the details that wrap us up and pin us down in our twenties. Life is about a single focus. "Seek first the Kingdom of God . . . Lay up for yourselves treasure in heaven . . . Enter by the narrow gate . . . Be like a wise man who built his house on the rock . . ." (Matthew 5–7). Each of these individual ideas points back to starting life with the same singular focus. We must make that choice because, as Maclaren says, we won't just drift into what is significant and right.

When we were in our twenties, Kelli and I chose God. And then we didn't. And then we chose God again. And then we got sidetracked. And then we did ministry for God without living intimately with God. And then we did dating. And then God slapped us alongside the head. Then God splashed our faces with cold water.

God reminds us daily that life is all about Him. We forget. Everything in the world is created by God and for God. That includes us. And *that* is what this book is about. It's about the constant choosing that God gives us in our twenties. We leave home, and we leave school, and God asks us to choose Him. It took Kelli and me awhile to develop some consistency. We'd love to share some of what we learned along the way.

—P. J. W.

OUR STORY: HINDSIGHT IS 20/20

This 20 Things idea began one year ago when I (Kelli) wrote an essay I didn't initially want to write.

I was on sabbatical from my teaching job at the time to try to write a book, one completely different book than this, mostly about the spiritual journey with all of its peaks and valleys, twists and turns. And I was afraid that brief essay would oversimplify some of the important ideas I hoped to unpack in a longer manuscript.

However, the more I tried to avoid that essay, the more it wrote itself in my heart and in my head—and the more I decided that it really ought to be.

See, Peter and I work with twentysomethings.

And we love so many things about them. Their vision and passion. Their honesty and creativity and courage. Their desire to change their world. But when we speak on their dormitory floors or invite them into our home for tea and talks, they often ask: "What is the most important piece of advice you would give to us?"

I'll be honest. I never answer well.

Dozens of thoughts start swirling around in my head, and I can never grab ahold of what I would deem to be the "most important" one. Instead, I just stutter and stammer and try to say something sensible. So on the surface that 20 Things essay was for anyone who had ever asked me that question and been disappointed.

Well, that essay I didn't want to write seemed to resonate enough so that now it is becoming a book of its own.

But here's the thing about that essay and this book. These 20 Things have truly grown out of our own journey with all of its peaks and valleys and twists and turns. These 20 Things have grown out of our own regrets, out of a gut-level compassion for who we were back then, from a wish that somehow we could step back through time, give our twentysomething selves a hug, shake our twentysomething shoulders at times, and sit down with our twentysomething selves for a long heart-to-heart over a skinny vanilla latte and a piece of chocolate cake.

Let us explain.

ME IN MY TWENTIES (KELLI)

I graduated from college at twenty-one with a communications degree and a dream. I felt called by God to go to Romania and tell people about Him—though I didn't know how or when or with whom. I shared this belief with the pastor of my home church in Minnesota. He was planning a five-week, solo summer mission trip for me, and I asked to spend at least part of that time with a Romanian pastor friend of his in Oradea.

A couple of months before the trip, however, my pastor

called me to explain that Romania was not going to work. I was scheduled to travel just a year and a half after the Romanian Revolution, and the country was still too unsettled. My pastor felt that it was too risky to send me there on my own. But, he said, I could go to the Netherlands and Germany instead. Not a bad backup plan at all.

So I went.

I spent a week serving in Holland and another week working in Germany. I was preparing to leave for Belgium when I received an unexpected invitation from a missionary to join a team he was leading into Romania in just a few days. I was stunned.

So unexpectedly I was able to spend two life-changing weeks in Romania, falling hard for the country and its people. It was the first time I had seen God move in such an extraordinary and surprising and powerfully personal way. And I was hooked—on all of it. I spent much of my twenties trying to get back to that place. Literally, back to Romania. Spiritually, back to that mission-trip "high."

At the end of that summer, I moved from Minneapolis to the Chicago suburbs to start my career and my grown-up life. A small Christian publishing house hired me to create a new children's church curriculum product for kids. The project got off to a good start. My boss believed in me, expanded my responsibilities, and even sent me to seminary.

I enrolled in Trinity Evangelical Divinity School, seeking a seminary education—and, truthfully, a seminary man. But, while I dated a bit, mostly I threw myself into my job, my studies, and my ministry at my new Chicago-area church. I sang in the choir, taught children's church, mentored the youth—became extra busy about God's work.

I moved into the upstairs apartment of a decrepit old house in downtown Wheaton. It was quirky and filthy when I first saw it. But it had wood floors and a claw-foot tub. Lots of "character." To me, it was ideal. I cleaned it up and painted every inch of the place. I decorated with inherited antiques and flea market finds and made for myself a quaint, cozy home.

And that's what I would have wanted you to see if you had come to visit.

A creative, independent, driven, ministry-minded twentysomething sort of girl.

However.

There were other things going on—beneath the surface and behind the scenes. Some of which I was aware. Others of which I was not.

Because, really, I wasn't just driven and busy. I was trying to prove myself and trying to add worth to my existence and to find happiness. I was filling my life to overflowing, so I didn't have time to think or feel too deeply or ask the hard questions or heal. I kept most of my friends at arm's length. I dated the wrong men. I tossed and turned many nights—trying to beat back loneliness, doubt, and fear. I wanted to own the faith I had been handed, but at the same time I wondered why it seemed that God kept slamming doors in my face. Why did He keep saying no to some of my deepest desires—like Romania and marriage and—as the decade wore on—a more fulfilling career?

Then, when I was twenty-eight, some doors—that had for so long been shut tight—finally started to swing.

I landed a teaching position at a Bible college. My dream job.

And I had only been on campus for one month when I met Peter. My dream man.

ME IN MY TWENTIES (PETER)

When I turned twenty, I was studying theology and philosophy at a college in Plymouth, England, where I am from. I was also training to teach primary (elementary) school.

Faith in God is floundering in England. Church attendance is plummeting. At my university, even my undergraduate theology professors rarely saw the inside of a church. In fact, they attacked the very existence of God and the reliability of the Bible. And when I tried to stand up for a biblical view of God, they humiliated me in classroom discussions. "No one believes that anymore," they said.

Still, I tried to hold on to my faith throughout those four long years. And finally, I graduated, a moral and intellectual mess. I was torn between the two worlds of belief and doubt. Hedonism (a love of pleasure) had a strong hold on me. And I had a love affair with romance. But—by the grace of God—I also had a seemingly irrepressible belief in Him.

Not long after I graduated from university, I left England to explore the world. My first base was Japan. I lived for three years in Tosayamada, a rural town where I taught English. As the only local Englishman, I was something of a celebrity. I was invited to many social events in town, made more money than I needed, and, with no obvious accountability, felt free to live my life as I pleased and for my own pleasure.

However, after those three years of indulging myself, I found that these things left me cold. I still sometimes enjoyed a good theological debate with my atheist friends in the local coffee shop. But, ironically, like my undergraduate professors, I rarely set foot in church. I knew I was standing on the edge of a dark abyss, peering into its depths. And I knew I had to pull myself away before I was sucked in completely.

So I decided to move again. This time to Pakistan, to teach at a Christian school in the foothills of the Himalayas—for $100 a month.

I enjoyed that mountain setting and the work, teaching and coaching the children. But because I tried to keep up with fashion and dressed accordingly, because I tried new teaching methods, and because I spent my free time playing soccer with the students, I soon became the subject of slander among my fellow missionary teachers and staff. Then the way I overreacted to a breakup with a girlfriend added fuel to their gossip fire.

In an effort to clear my head and regain perspective, I went into Afghanistan for a month. Trying to survive in a country marked with malnutrition, ravaged by civil war, and crippled by Taliban corruption soon brings the mind to focus. God showed me that my faith had been motivated by making life good for myself. I had been viewing God as a player in *my* story, and I had been frustrated when He didn't deliver the romance and the trinkets I thought I should have.

My time in Pakistan and Afghanistan also awakened my desire for more Bible training. So I enrolled in a master's degree program in Chicago to see if conservative theologians could unravel the tangled knots in my mind. The professors in the graduate school there were patient, intellectually diligent, and willing to converse with alternative ideas. They took me under their wing, and one of them even introduced me to a certain young professor named Kelli Ann.

US IN OUR THIRTIES

The story of how we met and dated varies considerably, depending on which one of us you talk to. This is my (Kelli's) version.

One bright September Friday, Peter was having lunch in the campus cafeteria with several of his classmates and a professor, Dr. Green. I wandered in and was looking lost and lonely in the salad bar line when Dr. Green recognized me from faculty orientation and took pity.

"Would you like to eat with me and some of my graduate students?" he asked.

Well, of course, I would.

Dr. Green led me to a long table, crowded with a dozen or so students. They shifted and created a space for me. Then they introduced themselves. Peter was seated next to Dr. Green.

In the middle of the meal, I overheard Peter tell another student—in his charming British accent—that Minneapolis, Minnesota, was his favorite city in the United States. Minneapolis is my hometown. Being the loyal Minnesotan that I am, I had to find out why this Brit was partial to it.

That was our first conversation.

Peter explained that his parents had lived in Minneapolis for a year while his dad did a teaching exchange. I explained that I grew up there. And we agreed on the city's best feature. The lakes. Peter asked me what I taught, and we discovered a shared love of literature and theater. And then, as I told him about the play I hoped to direct the following spring, he started smiling. One of those smirky smiles. As if he had some secret joke. I blushed and faltered and scrambled to recall what stupid thing I must have said. Then he jumped in to rescue me.

"I'm sorry," he said, all dimpled and brown-eyed and British, "but I just love your accent."

This is where our stories diverge.

I floated back to my office, grabbed my lesson plans, somehow found my class, and tried to form complete sentences. Later that afternoon, when I was packing up to go home, I pulled out my journal and jotted a few lines about that lunch. "I think I just met the man I am going to spend the rest of my life with." Then I added, "I can't believe I wrote that!"

Minutes later as I left my office building to catch a train, I looked across the lawn and there was—of all people—Peter. Sitting on a bench. With another girl.

So. For me, lunch that day was a divine introduction to my future spouse.

For Peter? At the time, not so much.

We ran into each other several times over the next few weeks, sat together at a missions conference session, lingered over dinners in the dining hall, talked all evening one Friday—at the end of which Peter walked me to my train.

After that, he started walking me to the train almost every day, and we would stop for coffee talks, which grew in both length and intensity as the weeks went on.

Eventually, I assumed that we were "dating."

And Peter? At the time, not so much.

Or so he claims.

One week before Christmas Peter showed up at my apartment unannounced. Since he was stranded in Chicago for the holidays, I had invited him to join me and my family in Minnesota. He had accepted the invitation, and we were planning to drive up in just a few days. However, on that surprise visit he came to tell me that he couldn't spend time with me any longer. The Other Girl on the bench ("just a friend") had encouraged him to cut ties with me, reminding him that he came to Chicago to focus on God, not girls.

I felt so many things. Pain, of course. Fear. Determination to handle this breakup better than I had some others. A desire to glorify God no matter what. And a strange assurance that this was not really the end.

I am a visual person, so I wrote on slips of paper—Peter, love, marriage, fear, and more. I struck a match and watched each piece burn in a bowl. I sacrificed my desires and my will on the altar.

Then I went to Minneapolis on my own.

Just a few days later, Peter got in touch. We reunited after the New Year, and thankfully he didn't run out the door when he asked about the bottle of ashes on my kitchen table and I said, "Well, that's you."

We spent a month in focused prayer for our relationship, both believing by the end of January that God had indeed brought us together for good reason.

That May Peter took me to England to meet his family. Then we worked side by side for the rest of the summer at a junior high day camp. One August night, Peter proposed. It wasn't a flashy affair. There wasn't even a ring. No diamond. No production. He just dropped to one knee in the middle of our nightly run. And asked, "Will you marry me?"

"Are you serious?" I said at first. I had imagined something a little more special.

"Yes," he said.

Then I said, "Of course."

At that point we believed that we could make it work. That we were allies and partners. Better together than we were apart.

The wedding was in England that Christmas. I was thirty. Peter was twenty-nine.

We started our fourth decade of life as husband and wife—full of anticipation and hope. For a couple of years, we lived the dream. I continued to teach. Peter took on a fifth-grade classroom and an administrative role at a Christian school. He was also invited to be the interim pastor at a small urban church. We bought a spacious 1920s condo in an artsy near-north suburb. And we made regular romantic weekend trips to quaint B&Bs.

However.

About three years into our marriage, the wheels began to wobble.

Peter's dad was diagnosed with pancreatic cancer. And died a short seven months later. He was only fifty-six.

Peter and I tried to start a family. But we were unable to get pregnant. Testing was inconclusive and treatments failed.

My parents—who both had cerebral palsy—were still in Minnesota, but they needed more and more help. They eventually decided to move to Illinois, and we bought a sizable home together with them. We were still getting settled when we found out that we were pregnant for the first time. A wonderful surprise. Then we lost the baby a few weeks later. It felt like the cruelest of jokes.

Two months after that, in the midst of major home renovations, we had a second pregnancy and miscarriage and a call from my mom to say that she had been diagnosed with cancer as well. Mom and Dad moved into our house at the end of the summer. We helped Mom through surgery in September and treatment throughout the next year.

Two years after they moved in, when Mom's cancer seemed to be at bay, my dad fell and broke his hip. His cerebral palsy and arthritis complicated the recovery, and it became impossible for us to care for him at home.

During all of this, Peter and I were also pursuing adoption. Our two-year China adoption process had turned into six. And while we waited, several other adoption possibilities fell through. We had dinner with one birth mom, then she chose a different couple. Another birth mom did choose us, took our $3,000, and disappeared without a trace. We provided a six-week safe home for one baby who was "probably going to be adoptable," but then her birth mom changed her mind. We were driving to the hospital to pick up another newborn when we received a call, informing us that this birth mom decided to tell the birth dad about the baby after all, and he was on a plane from Memphis. And so on. Blow after blow.

In the following spring, Mom's cancer returned. Dad's health was declining. And one day while I was meeting with the hospice nurse, receiving instructions on how to care for my mom in her final days, the nursing home called to recommend hospice care for my dad as well.

I collapsed into a chair—too incredulous to process it all and too numb to cry. After a few minutes, I willed myself to my feet, left my mom in the care of my mother-in-law, and drove across town to deal with my dad.

And that's what you would have seen if you had come for a visit.

A stressed, struggling, utterly-spent, thirtysomething sort of couple—holding a marriage and a family and a life together. But barely.

Yet, there were other things going on as well—beneath the surface and behind the scenes.

I (Kelli) was still trying to prove myself and add worth to my existence. I was still filling my life to overflowing so I didn't have time to think or feel too deeply or ask the hard questions or heal. I still kept friends at arm's length. I took Peter for granted and shut him out. I was still trying to beat back the pain and the loneliness and the doubt and the fear, screaming at God in anger for three years, crying out to Him in frantic desperation for another three. He seemed so silent.

I (Peter) wasn't in much better shape. I kept trying to talk with a wife who wasn't mentally or emotionally there. I kept trying to hold together a family in the only feeble ways I knew how. I shut down essential parts of my nature that I couldn't control. I stuffed and buried emotions and memories that I couldn't process—until they started to morph into dark thoughts and nightmares that were the beginnings of adjustment disorder, anxiety, and depression.

But here's the thing. While God brought us through that long, dark valley—and He has clearly used it for our good and His glory—we could have handled it better. We could have learned more quickly. And while He probably had these life events in store for us and that wouldn't have necessarily changed, we could have been better prepared. If only we had better understood these 20 Things.

Your twenties may look similar to ours—or they may look radically different. You may wander the world and relish repeated adventures, or you may settle down in some place safe. You may land a job quickly in your chosen field and begin the corporate climb, or you may wait tables and park cars and take your time figuring out what you really want to do. You may marry your college love and have babies before you know it, or—like we did— you may enjoy the independence (and simultaneously struggle with the solitude) of the single life.

But wherever you are and whatever you're doing, please don't underestimate the importance of this decade of your life. For in these pivotal years, you are charting a course. You are establishing a pattern. You are laying a foundation for the rest of your life.

ACTIONS TO CONSIDER

Make a "Life Map"—some sort of visual representation of the most formative experiences of your life. Be as creative as you care to be in its design.

Share your Life Map with someone (or a group of people) you trust.

QUESTIONS FOR REFLECTION AND DISCUSSION

- What have been the most formative experiences of your life thus far?
- How did these experiences shape you? What lessons did you learn (rightly or wrongly)?
- How did these experiences prepare you for adult life?
- Are there any lessons that you think you will need to "unlearn"?
- Where did you see God during these experiences? What did you learn about Him?

#1

EXAMINE YOUR FOUNDATION CAREFULLY

It's your worldview. Look deeply at what you value and what you believe about God and man and truth and reality. Then make it your own. Because it will affect every decision you make. Because life has a way of picking you up and tossing you around, and you always want to nail the landing.

What comes into our minds when we think about God is the most important thing about us.

—A.W. Tozer

We all have a worldview.

It's what we believe, not necessarily what we profess.

It's the ideas that actually control our lives—often without our realizing it. It's what drives our every thought, every decision, every move we make. It affects how we relate to other people, what we feel, and what we do under pressure. It informs how we spend our money and how we spend our time.

We come by our worldview effortlessly. We were helped in its construction—from the day we were born—by our families, our friends, our teachers, our experiences, our culture, our problems, and our faith.

To see how this happens, let's look at Mike.

Mike was raised in a suburban Christian home. For much of his life, his parents took him to sports every Saturday and to church every Sunday. He paid decent attention in Sunday school and youth group, and by the age of fourteen he thought he had most of the Christian thing figured out. Be nice to people. Read your Bible. And pray. Actually—if he was honest—Mike didn't really see the point to all of that Bible reading and prayer. It bored him. But he was as nice as the next guy.

In school Mike learned how to make sense of the world— through math and science, literature and history. He learned that the human race continues to evolve and progress. He learned that there is no ultimate authority, no single truth that applies to everyone for all time. Rather, he and his peers got to figure out what was true for them.

Mike learned about relationships from movies and music. He learned that men should be strong and assertive, that girls want a man who will make them feel good, and that having a girl by his side would make him feel good too.

Mike learned about happiness from advertising. In order to be happy, he needed the latest game system, the best car, the trendiest clothes, and the most money. And, of course, he needed to have the most fun.

When he arrived at college, Mike stopped attending that

suburban church. In fact, Mike stopped attending church much at all. He learned that sleeping in on Sunday mornings helped him recover from Saturday nights.

Mike's college friends came from all over the United States, even from all over the world. These new friends subtly influenced Mike's worldview. Although he had learned at his old suburban church that Muslims and atheists did not believe the truth about Jesus and would spend eternity separated from Him, the real Muslims and atheists he met were much nicer than he had imagined.

So, by his midtwenties, Mike was at a crossroads.

Before the cement of his worldview had even had a chance to cure, it had been placed under considerable pressure—at many points. And Mike was hardly even aware that it was happening.

EIGHT WORLDVIEW QUESTIONS

A few years ago I (Peter) sat down with a group of twentysomethings, and we developed this set of questions to help people identify their worldview:

1. Is there a supreme force, power, or being? If so, what is it like?
2. Is there a physical world, a spirit world, or neither?
3. Are human beings good, evil, or neither?
4. Is there such a thing as truth?
5. What do you value?
6. Can logic be trusted?
7. What books, people, or media inform your life?
8. What happens when people die?

Our answers to these eight questions will reveal—to a large degree—our worldview: Why we believe and feel and talk and act the way we do.

In answer to these eight questions, many people who grew up in a church (just like Mike) might say something like this . . .

"Sure, there's a God." They might acknowledge that He exists. However, they don't act as if He's terribly involved with the world—or with their life. They might pray in a time of undue stress, or even sing a Christian chorus (with arms raised?) if the opportunity presents itself. But God has little to do with their job or schoolwork or habits or hobbies or the way they interact with their family and friends. When people believe in such a distant God, they have to create their own purpose for living. They might decide that they want to live to serve others and make the world a better place. They might decide to focus on what feels good and to live for themselves and maybe their family. Or they may even decide that life is meaningless. They may even succumb to despair.

In answer to question #2, they might hem and haw and say, "I think there's a spirit world." But it doesn't matter much because they live in the here and now and trust their own senses. They are only aware of what they can see, hear, taste, touch, and smell, and they aren't worried about what might be going on behind the scenes.

MOST PEOPLE FIND THE QUESTION ABOUT TRUTH TO BE TRICKY.

In answer to question #3, many people who grew up in the church will say, "Of course, I'm good. Most people are." Then, if asked to define "good," they might say, "Nice." "Kind." "Not a jerk." And they would reserve "evil" for terrorists, murderers, human traffickers and such. And even then, they might hesitate to judge. After all, if those people were doing what they believed to be "right" and "true," who are we to pass blame?

Most people find the question about truth to be tricky. Some would say, "There is no such thing"—not realizing that this, in itself, is an assertion of truth. Others would say that truth is complex and unknowable. And if anyone claims to have it figured out, he must be arrogant or ignorant or intolerant or all of the above.

When asked what they value, many people might say, "Family. Friends. Work. Life. Health." Or they might say, "Authenticity. Selflessness. Justice. And peace." They might list all sorts of people and activities and objects and ideas. But the better question might be: Where do we spend our time and money and attention? Because that will reveal our actual values—whether we would name them as such or not. And while the things listed above are good, we also have to ask: When it comes to my life values, is "good" really "good enough"?

Many people also struggle with logic and its role. Historically, logic was central to learning. An hypothesis had to be researched and proven—with valid reasons and compelling evidence. However, our culture's standards today have shifted. Rather than requiring a solid argument, we now trust whoever tells the most heart-rending tale. Narrative trumps thought. Also, we feel obligated to give assent to absolutely everyone—no matter what they believe. To do otherwise—to engage with logic and to think critically—can be considered uncompassionate and cold.

When asked to name the sources that inform their lives, most people today find them too numerous to count. Certainly, family and friends still rank high on the list. However, their voices now compete to be heard over the hundreds of television stations and websites and billboard ads and celebrity promos and musical performances and Internet videos we encounter in a given week. And the indicator of whether or not something is worthwhile and credible is whether or not it went viral.

Finally, in answer to question #8, most people assume that their dead loved ones have gone to heaven and, of course, they themselves are headed there too. They might not use that exact term. But they comfort themselves with phrases like this: "I'll see him again" or "she's in a better place" or "he's looking down on me." And they believe that even people who had no time for Jesus on earth have gone to spend eternity with Him.

Christian Smith and Melinda Lundquist Denton gave a fancy name to the worldview we just described. It's "Post-Christian Moralistic Therapeutic Deism," and it's all the rage—in our culture and in many of our churches.[1]

However, it is something less than Christian.

A CHRIST-CENTERED WORLDVIEW

If we were to try to align our worldview with that of Christ, then it might look more like this . . .

We might say, Yes, there is a God. He is holy and sovereign and loving and unchanging. And He is intimately involved in every aspect of our lives. We live for His glory. And knowing Him changes absolutely everything.

Yes, there is a spirit world. It is the foundation of the world we can sense, and it permeates it at every point. It transcends the physical world as a giant transcends a ladybug.

Yes, I am evil. At least I was born that way. Now the evil person who came into the world can be crucified with Christ and a new person may live in her stead.

Yes, there is truth. And it is found in God and His Word and His world. And though none of us will ever come to understand it entirely, we will spend our lives seeking it out.

Yes, I value family and friends and other good things. But even more than those, I value God. All other things are a pile of dung compared to the value of knowing Him (Philippians 3:8).

Yes, I value logic. But my own logic pales in comparison to God's. He is all-knowing and perfectly reasonable, though He may not always seem so to us.

Yes, there is a heaven. And there is a hell. Heaven is a relationship with God—a loving God who does not force people to be with Him for eternity. So He has provided a second option. Eternal estrangement. We call that hell.

A FRACTURED FOUNDATION

When I (Kelli) was in my twenties, my worldview had some huge holes.

I believed a lot about God. I had already studied Him for years. And I thought I had Him all figured out. The theology that my church had handed me had hardly been questioned or challenged or truly made my own. God still fit in a nice God-sized box that I had set on the shelf. He was holy (check) and sovereign (check) and on down the list. He was also good, and He wanted good things for me. So if I delighted in Him, if I worked hard enough on His behalf, He would give me the desires of my heart. On demand. As far as I was concerned, that was the deal.

When I was in my twenties, I believed certain things about

human nature and about myself. Though I would have told you that people are sinful (evil) and are the grateful recipients of God's good grace, I had a hard time accepting that grace for myself. Secretly, I wanted to believe that I was pretty good, and I lived the tiresome life of a perfectionist—trying to perform; trying to live up to some unspoken, but powerfully perceived, expectations; trying to control my world. Grace was not sufficient and failure was not acceptable, so when I did fail—when I didn't get the job, when a mentee pushed me away, when a boy and I broke up—I couldn't forgive myself. Let alone accept forgiveness from God.

I spent most of my time at work and in ministry, with my friends, in seminary studies, and at the gym. I spent my small salary on coffee and clothes and quirky antiques—but also on mission trips and serving the teens from church. Certainly, I did value good things: people, service, education, health, and home. But truthfully, in hindsight, I think I mostly valued what these good things said about *me*. Their contribution to the identity and image *I* was seeking to create. And a more thorough inspection of my values may have revealed a preference for activity over intimacy, pleasure over purity, and spiritual ritual—small groups, quiet times, Bible memory—over real life change.

When I (Peter) was in my twenties, I believed that the Bible contained truth. But for me there were other truths as well. I held to a sacred/secular divide though I wasn't even aware of it. I could switch easily between these two worlds: one in which God existed, and one in which He did not. Biblical truth and scientific truth had no overlap in my mind. And though the borderline between the two realms was indistinct, it was there nonetheless. As a result, I led two lives. In my "secular" life, I taught in the public schools, partied with friends, and traveled the world. In my "sacred" life, I believed the truths that remained locked in the pages of Scripture. When I was in my twenties, I thought I was rational. I enjoyed a rousing debate in the corner coffee shop. However, I was rational like a French movie—dark and intellectual until love was involved. Then when a *femme fatale* entered the scene, I'd die a dramatic death on the stage of my own passion. I couldn't deny my heart, no matter how corny or melodramatic it seemed.

When I was in my twenties, the Internet had not yet been born, so I was influenced by books and music and movies. I read *The Sorrows of Young Werther* and watched *The English Patient*. These two works reinforced the darkness and fatalism surrounding my unrequited love. One was a classic piece of literature, and the other won Best Picture for 1996. So they *had* to be communicating truth, right? Not necessarily. I found out later that Napoleon banned his troops from reading *Werther* when too many love-sick soldiers were jumping off bridges rather than charging the enemy. *C'est la vie.*

Finally, when I was in my twenties, I believed that my destiny was a distant heaven. It may be a matter of some concern for the old and for the sick.

It makes sense, then, to do a thorough inspection—sooner rather than later.

But as a young and healthy soul, I was content to live in a vacuum until sometime in the far-off future when I might see Christ face-to-face.

INSPECTION TIME

So, the bottom line is this. We all arrive at our twenties with some sort of worldview in place. The forms were long ago built.

The concrete has been poured. But the material is still malleable.

Why does this matter?

Because, for the rest of our lives, it is upon this foundation that we build.

It makes sense, then, to do a thorough inspection—sooner rather than later.

It makes sense to allow God to examine your footings. To look for signs of structural failure. To identify the cracks. To drill down to bedrock and make thorough repairs—rather than settling for temporary remedies. In so doing, you will undoubtedly avoid some of the very costly repairs that can otherwise happen down the line.

ACTIONS TO CONSIDER

Ask your family and friends the eight questions from the beginning of this chapter.

Keep a careful log of where you spend your time and money for an entire week. What does this tell you about your values?

Re-watch your favorite movie or listen to your favorite music with the eight questions in mind. Ask: What worldview is being communicated?

QUESTIONS FOR REFLECTION AND DISCUSSION

- How would you answer the eight worldview questions from this chapter?
- Are you conscious of choosing a worldview? Or have you drifted into it?
- How do you see your worldview reflected in the way you live your life each day?

- Have you identified any areas where your worldview is not in harmony with God's design? If so, what are they?
- What might be the consequences of continuing down this worldview path?
- What might it look like to change how you think and act in this area? What steps might you take to change in this area?
- Ask God to reveal any places where He wants to address your worldview.

OTHER THINGS TO READ

Romans 12

Acts 17

Colossians 3

http://www.desiringgod.org/articles/when-your-twenties-are-darker-than-you-expected

Michael W. Goheen and Craig G. Bartholomew, *Living at the Crossroads: An Introduction to Christian Worldview* (Baker Academic).

J. P. Moreland and William Lane Craig, *Philosophical Foundations for a Christian Worldview* (InterVarsity).

Glenn S. Sunshine, *Why You Think the Way You Do: The Story of Western Worldviews from Rome to Home* (Zondervan).

#2

REMAIN
TEACHABLE

More specifically, find a mentor—a parent, a pastor, a teacher, a spiritual guide. Or just a person who is living as you would like to live. Spend time with them. Look and listen and learn. And, most important, be different because of them.

> *The fool doth think he is wise, but the wise man knows himself to be a fool.*
>
> —WILLIAM SHAKESPEARE, *AS YOU LIKE IT*

This morning our three-year-old daughter Amelia stood on her stool by the bathroom sink as I (Kelli) was drying my hair. For many minutes she tried with all of her might to pry open her precious Cinderella container, so she could fill it with water and "make tea." Seeing her struggle, I eventually reached toward her to help. At which point, she turned her back to me, shoulder high, shielding her project from my interfering touch.

"Momma, I can do it myself!" she claimed.

Our desire for self-sufficiency starts young, doesn't it?

When my hair was dry, I put the dryer away and walked down the hallway to our bedroom, leaving Amelia to wrestle—as requested—on her own. Moments later, I could hear the patter of her little feet running on the wooden floor. She'd had a change of heart.

"Momma! It's too hard. Can you open it please?" she asked.

Of course, I complied.

The first step in learning is realizing that we don't already know all there is to know. The first step in growth is opening up our minds and our lives to the wisdom of those who have gone before. The important first step in finding a mentor is admitting that we need help.

Mark Twain is often credited with saying, "When I was a boy of fourteen, my father was so ignorant I could hardly stand to have the old man around. But when I got to be twenty-one, I was astonished at how much the old man had learned in seven years."[1]

Unfortunately, some of us get stuck in that smug fourteen-year-old attitude. We cling to our self-sufficiency with three-year-old stubbornness, and we miss out on the many merits of having a mentor.

NOT A NEW PRACTICE

A second step in our journey of remaining teachable is to recognize that making deep, mutually valuable connections with someone who is further along than we are is an ancient practice. In the Old Testament, Moses mentored Joshua, and Elijah mentored Elisha. In both cases, the one who had essential skills and knowledge passed those things on to the one who followed behind.

In the New Testament, Paul mentored Timothy. Then in Titus chapter 2, he instructed us. He told older men and women to teach the younger how to act and how to speak. How to live and how to love.

In THE OLD TESTAMENT, MOSES MENTORED JOSHUA, AND ELIJAH MENTORED ELISHA. IN THE NEW TESTAMENT, PAUL MENTORED TIMOTHY.

And of course, in the Gospels, Jesus called His disciples to follow Him. There is no greater invitation to mentorship than that.

FINDING A MENTOR

Seeing, then, our need for mentors and the biblical pattern, how do we proceed?

A third step is to identify either a desirable strength in a person we know or a weakness in ourselves. It might be a basic life skill, like cooking or car repair. It might be a relational issue, such as how to solve conflict or how to date well. It might be a character quality, like patience or discernment or faith. Or it might be an area of knowledge, like computer programming or oil painting or the doctrine of propitiation. Alternatively—another, more general, approach is to simply identify a person we admire. Someone who is living as we would like to live in multiple ways.

The fourth step, then, is to make our need known. The main reason most of us don't receive mentorship is that we never ask. So we might invite our potential mentor to an initial meeting. Take him to dinner, or ask her to join us for a walk by the lake.

And just see how the conversation goes.

In their book *Connecting*, Paul D. Stanley and J. Robert Clinton explain that *attraction* is a "necessary starting point in the mentoring relationship."[2] In other words, the mentee should be drawn to the mentor's wisdom and character and ability to communicate. The mentor should see in the mentee a teachable spirit and opportunity to influence. Then, as the attraction between the two grows, so will the trust and the confidence and the connection.

If the initial meeting goes well and the potential for attraction is present, then we may articulate our desire in a more specific way. We might say, "I love your cooking, and I'm hopeless in the kitchen. Would you mind if I come over and watch you make a meal?" Or "I admire the relationship you have with your son, and I'm having a hard time relating to my parents. Would you have a couple of hours to help me think it through?" Or even "I'm struggling spiritually, and I don't know what to do. God seems so distant, but your relationship with Him seems compellingly intimate. Could we meet for an hour every Monday for the next eight weeks for accountability and prayer?"

Being this specific with our request—both with the time desired and the goal—helps our potential mentor make an informed decision and increases the likelihood that he or she will be able to say yes. Whereas a vague request—like "Will you mentor me?"—can sound daunting in its magnitude and ambiguity.

Admittedly, making such a vulnerable request is a risk. The response we receive may not be the one we want. Our desired mentor may not have the time. He may feel ill-equipped. She may feel that it's necessary to say no. Or not now. He may even agree to the arrangement and then fail to follow through. Disappointing scenarios, for sure. But don't let them discourage you or deter you from seeking out others and asking again.

In the meantime, though, another mentorship option is to read good books. There's this one, of course. (Wink, wink.) Once you've finished it, check out the suggestions at the end of each chapter for more ideas.

Whatever you do— keep looking for opportunities to learn.

Just—whatever you do—keep looking for opportunities to learn.

MENTORSHIP TAKES MANY FORMS

When I (Kelli) was in my twenties, I longed for a mentor, for one woman who would take me under her wing. I moved to the Chicago area right after college, knowing no one and feeling very alone. In the span of that decade, I asked a couple of women to mentor me. I met for a few times with each of them, but because I was unclear about my expectations—even in my own mind— the friendships fizzled and I was frustrated.

In hindsight, though, I see how I was looking for a particular person who would provide a depth of care that only God can. I also see how He *did* provide several people who each contributed to my growth.

He gave me a boss who taught me the ins and outs of curriculum development and the publishing world. There was the wife of the youth pastor, under whose leadership I served at church. She helped me settle into my wonky apartment in the upstairs of Gertrude Leaderman's ramshackle old house. She brought over her cleaning products and helped me wash the walls. She and her husband were models of a young couple in ministry. The mom of a good friend invited me over for Sunday lunches and holidays and showed me how to entertain with beauty and grace. There were seminary professors who taught me theology and pastors who helped me buy a car. And, too, I read my fair share of books.

And thus I was mentored. In many meaningful—albeit inadvertent—ways.

WHEN MENTORING WORKS WELL

A couple of years ago, Emma and Ian asked to meet with us. I already knew Emma, since she had been a student of mine and we had talked a number of times outside of class. I hadn't, however, met Ian. At that point, they had just graduated from college. They were both living and working in the city. Ian was about to start graduate school, and they had been dating for about a year.

They had talked about marriage quite quickly in their relationship. When they came to us, Emma was ready to get engaged. Ian, on the other hand, was feeling frightened. He loved Emma and saw a future with her, but every time they broached the subject of a possible timeline, Ian balked. His hesitancy fed Emma's insecurities, and she responded by building walls.

At our first meeting, they sat stiffly on our sofa.

We had them each explain their position. We asked hard questions, and they responded honestly. We made frank observations, and they received them with humility. They asked to come again. And we said, "Yes."

So every few weeks since then, they have made the long trip to our home in McHenry to be mentored. Sometimes they arrive beaming. Other times they arrive with boxing gloves on.

But always they arrive willing to work, ready to receive truth and grace, and eager to grow.

Last Christmas they called to share the happy news of their engagement. In June our whole family took a road trip to Texas, where Peter performed their wedding ceremony on a lovely ranch. This Christmas—since they were unable to travel to family—Emma and Ian spent the holiday in our home. Joining them on their journey has been both a blessing to us and a confirmation of the critical role of the mentor.

ACTIONS TO CONSIDER

Make a list of areas in which you require or desire growth.

Make a list of people you know who have the time and expertise to teach you.

Contact one person on your list for one meeting to start the conversation.

QUESTIONS FOR REFLECTION AND DISCUSSION

- Look at the biblical examples of mentorship mentioned in this chapter. What can you learn from each?
- Who has mentored you? In what way? To what effect?
- Do you have a mentor right now? If so, how is it going? If not, why not?
- Are there any books that have mentored you? In what way?
- If you don't currently have a mentor, ask God if He would have you pursue one.
- Who might you mentor?

OTHER THINGS TO READ

1 Timothy

1 Peter 5

John Calipari, *Swim to the Buoy: Why Everyone Needs the Safety of a Mentor* (Evergreen Press).

Daryl G. Donovan, *Men Mentoring Men* (CSS Publishing).

Bev Hislop, *Shepherding a Woman's Heart* (Moody).

Susan Hunt, *Spiritual Mothering: The Titus 2 Model for Women Mentoring Women* (Crossway).

Paul D. Stanley and J. Robert Clinton, *Connecting: The Mentoring Relationships You Need to Succeed in Life* (NavPress).

DIG DEEPER
THAN YOUR DOUBT

When waves of doubt rock your faith, don't panic. Don't despair. And don't jump ship without very careful consideration. Instead, voice your concerns. Seek answers to your questions. And when you get hold of the truth, hang on.

I am all in a sea of wonders. I doubt; I fear; I think strange things, which I dare not confess to my own soul.

—BRAM STOKER, *DRACULA*

I (Peter) used to teach a class for college seniors called the Philosophy of Christian School Education. It ran for three intense weeks every January and was specifically designed for those students who would spend the rest of their final semester as student teachers around the globe.

Students had to write a paper, in which they articulated what they believed now—at the end of their four-year Bible college career. Of course, many of them wrote straightforward essays.

Their beliefs lined up with the teachings from their theology courses: God was still God, people were born into sin, and salvation was offered by grace through Christ alone.

However, over the years, I also engaged with a stream of students who arrived at their senior year with doubts. Sometimes those doubts centered around the deity of Christ or the character of God or even His very existence. I appreciated it when these students let me know exactly where they stood, rather than write a paper with which they didn't fully agree. And rather than force them to be inauthentic, I always gave those students an extension on the assignment. Time for further inquiry and thought. In response, many of them launched into a cathartic conversation with me that lasted until they graduated, and sometimes beyond.

Take Christine, for example. She was visibly upset the first time she came to my office, trembling and on the verge of tears. "I don't know what's wrong with me," she said. When I probed, she told me that she had come to Bible college after serving in a camping ministry for a couple of years. At camp, she said, her faith had seemed so simple. She had prayed with campers and some had been saved. She had read the Bible with other counselors, and it had changed her life on a sometimes daily basis. Now—after four years of Bible college—that once beloved Word seemed like a dry textbook. She regularly felt anxious because she didn't know anymore if the Bible was even God's Word. And because she was no longer sure she could trust the Scripture to be true, she was no longer sure that Jesus was for real. And she wondered, then what?

MY OWN DOUBT

I empathize with those like Christine who come to me with doubt, because I have been there too. My faith started simple and small when I was very young. I accepted without question that the Bible was true and that Jesus died on the cross for my sins. I believed that real faith showed in good behavior and that my own behavior was good (enough).

When I got to high school, though, my peers started asking questions. If God created everything, then who created God? How can we know the Bible is true? How do we know God exists? Each time I fielded one of these questions, I went to the adults in my church, and they gave me ready answers—which I, in turn, passed on. These answers seemed to satisfy, and several of my friends even gave their lives to Christ. As a result, I must admit, I got cocky. I thought I knew everything there was to know about the Bible and Christianity. I had no idea that I had only scratched the surface.

When I was in my twenties, my faith really came under attack. While I was serving in Pakistan, other missionaries—who seemed much smarter and more experienced than I was—questioned the reliability of the Bible. They challenged me regarding the age of the earth. And they quoted Karl Barth and others to reinforce their ideas.

In Pakistan I also saw much more the effects of evil on the world. Children crippled by their parents so they could gain more money begging. Drugs and guns sold freely over the counter in a lawless northwestern town. And as most of us do at some point in our lives, I asked, Why, God? If You are all-powerful *and* You are good—why?

Then the attacks on my faith seemed to get more personal. When I was younger, there had been a friendly air of inquiry when my friends and I talked about what we believed. But as I moved through my twenties, people of faith were more frequently marginalized—called morons, backward, or just plain ignorant. I didn't want to be any of those things, so it seemed safer to doubt.

A COMMON PHENOMENON

Doubt is not a twenty-first-century issue. Even in the Bible we read about men and women who found it difficult to believe God at times. Sarah and Abraham laughed at His promise (Genesis 17–18). Gideon tested Him twice before he would trust (Judges 6). And, of course, Doubting Thomas's disbelief of the resurrection earned him that unfortunate nickname (John 20).

However, even though doubt has been around for centuries, our current culture *does* create a particularly "doubt-inducing" environment. In their book *In Search of a Confident Faith*, J. P. Moreland and Klaus Issler identify several popular presuppositions that even Christians today often absorb. From our modern media and education and conversation, we learn the following:

- It is smarter to doubt things than to believe them.
- We can know things only through our five senses (and through science).
- Enlightened people are tolerant, nonjudgmental, and compassionate.[1]

When these ideas seep into our subconscious, they can easily eat away at the foundation of our faith. Skepticism seems more sophisticated than faith. We feel foolish for believing in something we cannot see or hear or touch or otherwise prove with empirical evidence. Then we see that the absolute nature of many biblical claims is unpopular, and therefore embarrassing. And doubt creeps in.

If any of this describes your journey, you are certainly not alone.

In a book cowritten with his father (*The Post-Church Christian*), Carson Nyquist describes his generation in general as "skeptical," marked by doubt and cynicism.[2] He attributes this stance, in part, to the failings of CEOs and pastors and priests, who were very publically charged with scams and scandals. "Much of what we experienced [growing up]," Nyquist writes, "fell short of what was promised. And so we doubted. Some of us doubted our faith; others, our churches; others, our families. We doubted their love for us, their motivations, their stories, and their advice."[3]

Sean McDowell, son of the renowned apologist Josh McDowell, has also been open about his season of doubt. At a recent conference for Christian educators, I heard the younger McDowell give an energetic presentation on worldview. Listening to him that afternoon, I assumed that he had been carefully groomed by his father. I imagined that, growing up in such a family, he must have been handed a nicely packaged, well-reasoned—and consequently unquestionable—faith. I was surprised to later discover that this was not the case.

In "When Kids Question Their Faith," Josh and Sean McDowell describe the awkward conversation that had to happen after Sean went away to college. He took a class called Authentic Manhood, which challenged him to honestly address his father's shortcomings in order to love him more fully. Simultaneously, Sean discovered several websites that challenged the arguments of his father's book *Evidence That Demands a Verdict.* Together these attacks on his worldview unsettled him. He said, "I hit a point in my life—as many young people do—where I was asking deep intellectual and existential questions. And it wasn't enough for me to believe something because my parents did. I had to find the truth for myself."[4]

WHEN DOUBT COMES

People like Christine still come to me, and I often begin by just letting them unwind. They may have to cry and release the many levels of fear that can accompany their doubts: fear about what other people will think—of rejection, of wasting a Bible college education, of not being able to discern what is right. Fear about their identity and losing their faith altogether. I assure them that I will accept them no matter what they believe. I also tell them that the essay they are writing for my class is an academic assessment, not a religious one. And if they express disagreement with our school's doctrine, they can still pass the course. It's interesting how even the removal of that simple obstacle helps give students permission to

Sometimes students simply haven't processed their faith deeply enough. They have been told so much, so rapidly, that they are suffering from spiritual indigestion.

doubt. Suddenly, their shoulders relax, and they start to reflect.

Our faith needs to catch its breath sometimes. Sometimes we receive so many truths in quick succession that we don't have time to sort them out. When this happens, it is common for doubt, or even outright rejection, of the beliefs to occur—simply because truth can take time to properly digest. Of course, during a reflective process, we may realize that we *have* been taught something in error and we *do* have to reject it.

In the case of my students, though, they sometimes simply haven't processed their faith deeply enough. They have been told so much, so rapidly, that they are suffering from spiritual indigestion. My role, in part, is to give them permission to break down and absorb what they have been asked to consume.

So the first thing I encourage people to do with their doubt is to pay attention. Don't ignore it or hide it or try to pray it away. Timothy Keller issues this word of warning to anyone who wants to overlook these important matters of faith: "People who blithely go through life too busy or indifferent to ask hard questions about why they believe as they do will find themselves defenseless against either the experience of tragedy or the probing questions of a smart skeptic."[5] In other words, if we don't deal with our doubt, we leave ourselves open to any attack. Carson Nyquist agrees, and he reiterates that this process is invaluable. In fact, he goes so far as to say that "doubt *should* be a part of our faith. Without it, we are simply accepting truth as fact, not thinking for ourselves."[6] Thus, acknowledge your uncertainty, own the process of investigation, and prepare to give your faith the time and thought that it deserves.

Second, clearly articulate your concerns. Give voice to your doubt. Perhaps begin by journaling. But sooner, rather than later, bring your questions to people you can trust. Some of my students who express their doubts in my office continue the conversation with me. Many talk with their pastors, mentors, parents, or reliable friends. Some actually watch their doubts dissolve when I simply help them process and release the related negative emotions—shame, anger, resentment—that have built up over time.

Others are pleasantly surprised when they share their doubts with their elders. They are surprised by the gracious reception, open conversation, and helpful advice. How do you think Josh McDowell handled the news when his son Sean came to him? Josh was not particularly surprised. He assured his son that he loved him very much, no matter what he believed, and he gave Sean his blessing to question the faith. Then Josh had two pieces of counsel for his son. "First, I told him that if he honestly sought the truth, he would find it. Second, I told him not to reject something simply because it was part of his parents' faith."[7]

> I was completely unaware of the wealth of resources that are available to Christians who want to understand and defend a more conservative faith.

Which brings me to my third point. Dig deep. Search for truth. Find well-reasoned resources that stretch your thinking and answer your questions and fairly address the opposing views. When I was in my twenties and my faith was under attack, I was largely on my own. I had to read lots of liberal theology for my undergrad studies—Bultmann, Rahner, and Küng. My questions had become too complex for the elders at my church. And I was completely unaware of the wealth of resources that are available to Christians who want to understand and defend a more conservative faith. I had never heard of Ravi Zacharias, William Lane Craig, or R. C. Sproul. As a result, my twentysomething life with Christ was riddled with doubts like a poorly kept field is strewn with weeds. And I didn't have the tools to dig up the weeds so my faith could grow in any healthy fashion.

It wasn't until I came to America for graduate school at the age of twenty-eight that I met people who had more thorough ways of addressing doubt. They engaged wholeheartedly with the process, they sought out others who had insight, they found good books that dug deep, and they encouraged me to do the same.

I believe that the truth of a biblical faith can withstand the growing pains of a reflective mind. I've seen it happen for students like Christine. I've heard how it happened for Sean McDowell. And I have experienced it myself.

DEAL WITH DOUBT IN RELATIONSHIP

If we approach our faith merely like an academic exercise, or like a list of bulleted theological points to which we give our intellectual assent, then it might seem relatively easy—when doubt creeps in—to delete the document and replace it with something else. But adhering to Christianity does not just mean affirming a particular creed. Our faith is a relationship with the triune God. Therefore, our doubts must be handled in a relational way—not just an academic one.

When doubt comes—in any relationship—we can address our concerns in conversation. But perhaps the best way to reconnect, to rebuild trust, is to spend time.

We can see Jeremiah do this in the book of Lamentations. If you haven't read the whole book, you only need to read a few verses to catch the tone. Jerusalem has fallen. Jeremiah has witnessed unspeakable horrors. And for most of the book's five chapters, he pours his grief and his doubt out to God—a God who, according to Jeremiah, "brought [him] into darkness without any light" (Lamentations 3:2). Jeremiah says, "Surely against me he turns his hand again and again the whole day long" (3:3). And then, "He drove into my kidneys the arrows of his quiver" (3:13). Ouch. That's got to hurt. On and on Jeremiah laments.

Until we get to the very middle of the book. And we hear Jeremiah say,

> But this I call to mind, and therefore I have hope: The steadfast love of the LORD never ceases; his mercies never come to an end; they are new every morning; great is your faithfulness. "The LORD is my portion," says my soul, "therefore I will hope in him."
>
> The LORD is good to those who wait for him, to the soul who seeks him. (3:21–25)

In the midst of calamity and fear, Jeremiah recalls the faithfulness of God. It is a ray of light that brings him hope—hope that there may be a way back to peace with God. Of course, after these verses, the book of Lamentations descends once more into anguish and tears. But such is sometimes the reality when we wrestle with doubt and simultaneously seek love.

If someone we love is far from us, we seek out him or her. In similar fashion, if God seems hidden from us, we should seek His face. When the God we have known seemingly disappears from view, when He descends over the horizons of our doubt or our disappointment, we must move. We ought to follow Him into the darkness until He leads us into a new day. We must remind ourselves that His love never ceases. His mercies are new every morning. And He will reveal Himself in new measure at the dawn.

ACTIONS TO CONSIDER

If you are wrestling with doubt, put into writing your questions and concerns about your faith.

Identify someone you can express your doubts to. Set up a time to meet with him or her.

Make a list of books or other resources that address your particular questions. Don't hesitate to contact people you respect for their expertise, and ask them for recommendations.

QUESTIONS FOR REFLECTION AND DISCUSSION

- Have you ever experienced a period of doubt? If so, describe it.
- Are you struggling with doubt right now? If so, explain.
- How does it feel to doubt? Have you been able to release the negative emotion that often surrounds doubt?
- How have you seen doubt handled by the church?
- Have you discussed your doubt with someone? Describe that experience.
- How can you support someone else who is struggling with doubt?
- What would "digging deeper" look like for you?
- What will you do to spend time with God as you seek Him?

OTHER THINGS TO READ

Lamentations

J. P. Moreland and Klaus Issler, *In Search of a Confident Faith* (IVP).

J. Paul Nyquist and Carson Nyquist, *The Post-Church Christian* (Moody).

Barnabas Piper, *Help My Unbelief: Why Doubt Is Not the Enemy of Faith* (David C. Cook).

www.seanmcdowell.org/index.php/youth-culture/when-kids-question-their-faith.

http://rzim.org/ (Ravi Zacharias International Ministries).

www.thegospelcoalition.org/article/doubting-your-doubts.

www.thegospelcoalition.org/article/dealing-with-the-doubting.

www.thegospelcoalition.org/article/the-faith-to-doubt-christianity.

#4

CHOOSE YOUR
COMMUNITY
CAREFULLY

Your friends will give shape to your life. They will either stunt your growth or spur you on. And when you find good friends, keep them. They are like gold. Treasure them. Invest in them. Spur them on too. Be the kind of friend that you would like to have.

You can't stay in your corner of the Forest waiting for others to come to you. You have to go to them sometimes.
—A.A. MILNE, *WINNIE THE POOH*

We are more connected, more plugged in, more in touch with one another than ever before.

From our handheld devices, we can text and email and message no matter where we are—at work, at school, at church—while we're sitting in a parking lot, or sipping a latte on a "real live" coffee date. In our pocket or in our purse, we have at our fingertips a fantastic number of followers and friends—at least "friends" of the "I favorite your photo, you like my status" variety. But how does our uber-connectedness affect our ability to really relate? Sherry Turkle says that we are increasingly "alone together."[1]

As an MIT Professor, Turkle has studied the effects of technology on our lives, and according to her research, we crave connection as much as human beings ever have—but we now want it in our own customizable way. We want complete control over the image we present and the amount of attention we afford. And because real conversation is often unpredictable and inefficient, we no longer prioritize meeting with one another in real time and in real space. Why should we? "Now we look to the network to defend us against loneliness even as we use it to control the intensity of our connections," says Turkle. "Technology makes it easy to communicate when we wish and to disengage at will."[2] So we opt, then, for superficial and sporadic connection instead of deep and abiding intimacy.

CREATED FOR COMMUNITY

Technology, in and of itself, is not the problem though. Even Turkle admits that technology offers many pluses, and it certainly has its place. It just makes true community in the twenty-first century a bit more complicated to construct.

It's important for us to understand, though, that—even in our hyperconnected society—creating and maintaining true community is still critical.

The human need for community can be traced all the way

back to the beginning of time. We see it in the very nature of our triune God—Father, Son, and Holy Spirit. We see it in the way that He created the first human being in His image and then declared, "It is not good that the man should be alone" (Genesis 2:18). We see it in the many commands throughout Scripture regarding how we are to treat one another—preferring one another, forgiving one another, living in peace. We see it in the way Jesus called His twelve disciples to follow Him, in the way God gifted us in complementary ways as the body of Christ, and in the way He established His church to carry out His mission on earth.

There's no doubt. We are created for community.

WHAT THE EXPERTS SAY

But what role does community play in our lives? We may agree that God ordained it to be, but why? What difference does it make? What does community do for us?

Many experts—both Christian and non—have sought to answer these questions. Here's what a few of them have to say . . .

In the first half of the twentieth century, Erik Erikson identified eight stages in a person's "psychosocial development." During our teenage years, Erikson said, we are trying to figure out who we are and to whom we belong. If we complete this stage well, we enter our twenties with a strong and well-formed personal identity. On the other hand, if we struggle through our teens, if we aren't given the guidance we need to figure out what we believe and where we are to go, we will likely enter our twenties full of ambiguity and confusion—about our own self and our place in the world.

In community, we come to understand ourselves and others. In community, we come to understand the world.

According to Erikson, our young adult years ought to be a time when relationships deepen, requiring of us a new level of love and care and sacrifice. It ought to be a time of increased intimacy. But for those of us who arrive at our twenties with a poor sense of self, it is often instead a time of isolation. And, as James Wilhoit and John Dettoni observe, if we don't first know who we are, we can't begin to give ourselves away.[3]

In community, then—bottom line—we come to understand ourselves and others.

Jean Piaget, a contemporary of Erikson, proposed his own influential theory, which sought to explain how we learn. He laid out four major stages of cognitive development that span birth to adulthood. But what is most pertinent to this conversation is that, for Piaget, learning at all four stages is primarily a social activity. It is in the context of relationships that we mature—as we wrestle with ideas and overcome obstacles.

In community, then—bottom line—we come to understand the world.

In the 1950s, Lawrence Kohlberg built his research on the work of Piaget. He explored the development of our moral reasoning and identified three levels.

In Level I, as children, we are influenced primarily by the commands of adults and by their administration of punishments or rewards. In Level II, as we mature, we look to the important people in our lives to guide our moral understanding. We make decisions because we want to please others and be seen as a good person. Then—finally—in Level III, we operate more by principles, which we have owned and internalized. We do the right thing simply because it is the right thing. Unfortunately though, according to Kohlberg, most adults never grow beyond Level II, and they remain primarily people pleasers.

Regardless, it is in community that we realize what is right and what is wrong.

James Fowler was a colleague of Kohlberg and was influenced by his work. But Fowler sought to explain people's journey of faith. For Fowler, "faith" was a general term. We all have faith, Fowler said, because we all believe in something.[4] What he was concerned with was not *what* we believe, but *how.*

Fowler, too, used stages to explain the progression—six stages to be exact. And although they are a bit complicated, what is clear—once again—is the role of relationship. Key to the development of our beliefs are the adults in our lives, the groups with whom we gather, and the peers who help us process.

In community, then—bottom line—we figure out our faith.

And thus, in many ways and for many reasons, the friends you keep are crucial.

WHEN COMMUNITY IS GOOD

For three years, when I (Peter) was in my midtwenties, I lived in Japan. I was teaching English, making more money than necessary, and living a relatively carefree life. I had a few Western friends, and often at midnight we would finish our evening of karaoke and hit the still-busy streets of Kochi, looking for something more to do. Regularly my friend Aaron and I would end up in the same place—the base of Kochi-jo, otherwise known as Kochi Castle. Unlike the towering stone walls of European castles, the walls of Kochi Castle sloped. Once we crossed the former moat, we could climb the walls with ease. So many nights Aaron and I raced up the walls of the castle and back down again. It's amazing what your friends can persuade you to do.

Aaron was a gracious and thoughtful atheist. He and I debated the existence of God in a bright yellow and orange coffee shop called Pumpkin. He sharpened my thinking in many ways, and he certainly influenced my development during my time in Japan.

W HAT DOES A TRULY GREAT COMMUNITY LOOK LIKE? AND HOW can we acquire one?

However, what Aaron didn't do—what he couldn't do—was draw me closer to God. Yes, God did use him in my life in some ways, but God was not his focus and our true communion was limited. Aaron was a good friend. But sometimes good is the enemy of great.

WHEN COMMUNITY IS GREAT

Even though God *can* use friends of many descriptions for the good, our friendships that are not reflecting God's grace can leave us satisfied with something less than great. To clarify, we aren't suggesting that you should *only* have Christian friends. But we *are* saying that you ought to have a great community around you.

What, then, does a truly great community look like? And how can we acquire one?

First of all, we can investigate the life of Jesus. He's the ultimate example of a friend. He was compassionate and loyal, intentional and dangerous. He pursued people of all persuasions—

from fishermen to religious leaders, from prostitutes to the sick. The messiness didn't matter. What was key was a person's desire to know Him and to grow, to leave behind their slavery to sin and follow Him. To those people He generously gave of His time and His resources. He sat with them. He asked questions, and He listened. He challenged their thinking, and He spoke the truth in love. He offered healing and invited them to commune at the foot of the cross. Let's learn from Him.

Second, let's initiate. Sometimes it is simply our own fear that keeps us from friendship. So let's take the risk, and be the first to reach out. Rather than protecting ourselves from potential pain, let's pursue people—of various persuasions. Invite them in. Sit with them. Ask them questions and really listen to their response. Let's take the time to till the soil, and the fruit may well be a newfound friend.

Third, let's invest wisely. Many people and projects vie for our attention each day. And we must make choices about where to invest our time and attention. Sometimes we feel stuck in a relationship that is simply wrong. We have to keep coming back to the key question: Am I drawing this person closer to Jesus? And/or is this person doing the same for me? If the answer is yes, pour yourself in. Give generously. Love lavishly—just like Jesus. But also—just like Jesus did—learn to say no when necessary.

Finally, let's implement our own ideals. Let's be the kind of friend we would want to have. Last week we did an informal online survey and we got nearly a hundred responses. We asked: "What is the most important quality you look for in a friend?" Topping the list was loyalty and unconditional love, with honesty and trustworthiness and transparency following close behind. Jesus was all of these things. Let us be too.

"COMMUNITAS," NOT COMMUNITY

Images of community are present in just about every adventure series you can name. *Star Wars. Matrix. Lord of the Rings.* And we love these stories. We are drawn into the journey, the quest, and the need to survive. But, too, the sense of comradeship calls to us, that image of a group of people banding together around a common goal. This is community at its best.

But this sort of community is hard to find in our culture, a culture which values safety and security and stability over sacrifice. We prefer comfort and convenience over anything costly. We are individualistic and competitive. And in order for us to win, we accept that those around us will lose. As Alan Hirsch explains in his book about the missional church, we live as if the community should serve us. Not as if we should serve the community.[5]

As an example of what community can be, Hirsch describes a rite of passage ritual among certain African people groups. In some tribes, the younger boys are cared for by the women until the age of thirteen. When the time of initiation has come, the men come into the female compound at night and kidnap the boys. They are blindfolded and taken out into the African bush where they are left to fend for themselves for up to six months. Periodically, elders of the tribe meet with the boys and mentor them. But for the most part, they are left to their own devices, and they have to band together—developing both individual and communal strength in order to survive.[6] By necessity, they build "communitas"—a level of sharing and intimacy that comes when a group of people experiences a significant transition together.

For many of us, our twenties feel something like this adventure in the African bush. Unfamiliar and frightening. But if we choose our community carefully, if we band together around our common goal, if we submit to one another in humility and love, we too can create "communitas."

ACTIONS TO CONSIDER

Take a weeklong fast from social media—or even all technology, if possible—and invest that time in your face-to-face friendships. What does this exercise reveal about the benefits and challenges of social media and technology?

Consider inviting people to your home. Choose a topic to discuss or an activity to engage in. See what happens. Can this be a regular thing?

QUESTIONS FOR REFLECTION AND DISCUSSION

- What sort of community do you have right now?
- Do they draw you closer to Jesus? In what ways?
- Do you draw them closer to Jesus? In what ways?
- Do you need to initiate in any friendships right now? If so, how and when will you do this?
- Are you investing your relational time and energy wisely? Ask God to show you if any changes need to happen. Do you need to say "no" to anyone right now?
- Are you being the kind of friend you would like to have? If so, how? If not, what needs to change?
- What would "communitas" look like in your life right now?

OTHER THINGS TO READ

Proverbs 13

Romans 12

Alan Hirsch, *The Forgotten Ways: Reactivating the Missional Church* (Brazos).

Anne Marie Miller, *Lean On Me: Finding Intentional, Vulnerable, and Consistent Community* (W Publishing).

Kyle Tennant, *Unfriend Yourself: Three Days to Detox, Discern, and Decide about Social Media* (Moody).

Sherry Turkle, *Alone Together: Why We Expect More from Technology and Less from Each Other* (Basic Books).

James C. Wilhoit, *Spiritual Formation as if the Church Mattered: Growing in Christ through Community* (Baker Academic).

#5

FEED
YOURSELF

Feed your body, your mind, and especially your soul. When your soul is starving, you can't see straight. So learn what sort of nourishment you need: a group Bible study? a worship song? a long run? an art project? a prayer with a friend? This is an individual matter, so take the time to figure out what fills you up.

Tell me what you eat and I will tell you what you are.

—ANTHELME BRILLAT-SAVARIN

I (Kelli) am writing this on January 2, and—like most of America—I put "feed myself better" near the top of my resolution list yet again this year. The holidays in our house are always deliciously destructive.

Last week, among other things, Peter made his English apple pie—the one with orange and lemon rind and an excessive amount of salt right in the crust. The one that is perfectly complemented by dulce de leche ice cream. The one that has officially ruined all other pies for me.

Then, multiple times, my mother-in-law made her famous caramel shortbread—the one that begins with a layer of melt-in-your-mouth shortbread, that is topped with a layer of gooey homemade caramel, that is topped with a thick layer of creamy milk chocolate. The one that all of our friends frequently demand. The recipe for which she has distributed countless times.

Because I have an insatiable sweet tooth, I devoured more than my share of both delectable desserts. Yes, I did what all of us do—so much of the time. I chose the pleasure of the moment over the reality of the long-term consequences. And here I am, at the start of a new year, feeling once again weighed down and sluggish and full of regret.

SUPER SIZE ME

You may have seen the award-winning documentary *Super Size Me* by independent filmmaker Morgan Spurlock. Over Thanksgiving weekend in 2002, Morgan saw a news broadcast about two teenage girls who had sued the fast food giant McDonald's. The girls claimed that they became obese as a result of the addictive and physically harmful nature of the chain's food. The girls lost the case.

But Morgan was both intrigued and enraged when he heard McDonald's representatives respond to the allegations. They defended their product and asserted that their food was "healthy."

"If that's true," Morgan told his then-girlfriend, "I should be able to eat it for three meals every day with no adverse effects." Thus, the *Super Size Me* film project was born.

For thirty days—from February 1 to March 2, 2003—
Morgan ate at McDonald's restaurants for every meal. He tried
every menu item at least once. He consumed an average of five
thousand calories per day. He gained 24½ pounds. His choles-
terol shot up. Fat accumulated on his liver. He suffered from leth-
argy and headaches and depression.

On day twenty-one, his doctor advised him to abandon the
project because of heart palpitations and a concern that his body
was suffering surprising and significant damage. But Morgan
continued and completed his goal, raising awareness about
two of our country's biggest health issues: fast food addiction
and obesity.[1] According to *The Journal of the American Medical
Association*, the rate of obesity in America has risen dramatically
over the past twenty years so that currently over 34 percent of
adults and 17 percent of children fall into that category.[2]

However, while stuffing ourselves with unhealthy food is
one of our nation's prevalent eating problems, another is starving
ourselves of food. For some of us, "super-size" means small. The
statistics on this are also staggering. The website for the National
Association of Anorexia Nervosa and Associated Disorders offers the following collection of data and paints this problematic
picture:

- Up to 24 million people of all ages and genders suffer
  from an eating disorder in the US.[3]
- 25% of college-age women engage in bingeing and
  purging as a weight-management technique.[4]
- Over 50% of teenage girls and 33% of teenage boys
  use unhealthy weight control behaviors—such as

skipping meals, fasting, smoking cigarettes, vomiting, and taking laxatives.[5]

- Eating disorders have the highest mortality rate of any mental illness.[6]
- 20% of people suffering from anorexia will die prematurely from complications related to their eating disorder, including suicide and heart problems.[7]

When we don't give our body enough to eat, the effects are enormous. Our metabolism slows. Our immune system is weakened. Our muscles disintegrate. Our body swells. Our heart is damaged. And eventually our brain function is impaired.

Thus, we see our human tendency toward excess or extreme—toward either a fatty feast or a famine. Thus, we see the widespread struggle to feed ourselves well—because healthy eating is surprisingly hard work.

I (Peter) was raised in a working-class home where each meal was evaluated by its quantity rather than its quality. On the rare occasion when we went out to eat, my father's favorite was an all-you-can-eat pizza bar, and he would get annoyed if my mother and I didn't stuff ourselves to the gills. He had to get his money's worth.

My family also taught me that it's a waste, even a crime, to leave food on my plate. So when I was in my twenties and I spent two years of graduate school eating at the all-you-can-eat campus cafeteria, I had no self-control and I gained forty pounds. I couldn't run as fast. My clothes didn't fit, and I didn't feel well. Period.

A few months after I graduated, I went for a routine medical appointment during which my doctor gave me a wake-up call and told me my healthy target weight. I left her office in a bit of shock but resolved to figure out how to feed myself well.

I didn't follow a fad diet. Instead, I ate sensible foods in sensible portions several times each day. I added additional exercise to my routine, and I lost about four pounds per week. It took me many months, but I eventually hit my target weight and stopped. Lighter, fitter, healthier, and happier. On the one hand, it was a simple approach. On the other hand, it required a level of discipline that was very difficult to sustain. I failed often, suffering several setbacks. But the bottom line was this: it took me some time to figure out what my body needed to achieve a measure of health. And it took great effort to act on that knowledge.

A HEALTHY MIND

Some of the same truths that apply to feeding our bodies also apply to feeding our minds. Our brain is like a muscle. The more we nourish it and exercise it, the stronger it will grow. Unfortunately—mentally—many of us are starving, and many of us consume large quantities of empty calories.

While one might assume that—in this Information Age— our seemingly unlimited access to knowledge is making us smarter than ever before, many fear that quite the opposite is true. In 2008 Nicholas Carr wrote a popular article for *The Atlantic* magazine. He called it "Is Google Making Us Stupid?" and he built a compelling case for the idea that our increasing Internet use not only affects our access to information, it also affects what our brain does with it. Because our twenty-first-century minds are being conditioned to skim the surface of so many search engine results and social media feeds, Carr fears that we are losing our ability to concentrate and contemplate and critically

Can we any longer converse about complicated topics? We find it difficult to read and understand an entire article, let alone a whole book.

evaluate. Can we any longer converse about complicated topics? We find it difficult to read and understand an entire article, let alone a whole book. What we have gained in breadth, Carr argues, we have lost in depth.[8]

What then can we do?

J. P. Moreland suggests that one of the best ways to develop our thinking—and to love God with our mind—is to read books.[9] Good books. Classic books. Beautiful, well-crafted books. Books that are increasingly complex. Books that challenge our thinking and dig a little deeper than our current understanding. Books that stretch our brains. Each time we read a good book, we build a bit of scaffolding around our mind so that we can climb a little higher. And a little higher again. Then a little higher still.

Loving God with our mind might also mean taking a class or attending a conference or learning a new skill or joining a discussion group at our local library. It might mean visiting a museum or playing a strategic game or researching and discussing with friends an interesting topic about which we've always wondered.

Loving God with our mind can look many ways.

Try one and watch what a difference it can make.

FEEDING OUR SOULS

Finally, the way we nourish our body and our mind also affects the nourishment of our soul. These areas of our lives are interconnected. What we eat is not just a physical choice, it is also a spiritual one. Where we choose to focus our mind is not just a cognitive decision, it is a spiritual one as well. All health affects our spiritual health. All valuable growth is spiritual growth. We dare not try to divide them. And our twenties is an important time to understand this truth and take ownership of all of it. It's an important time to learn to feed ourselves—body, mind, and soul.

When it comes to feeding our soul, however, our biggest problem may not be intentional stuffing or starving. Our biggest problem may simply be neglect. We may not see soul care as a need. We may not recognize those hunger pangs. We may wait passively for others to provide the nourishment that we need—our pastor, our parents, our teachers, or our friends. We may be so busy that we just don't take the time. And our soul slowly shrivels.

What, then, does a well-fed soul look like? How do we feed our own?

I (Kelli) regularly revisit the image in Psalm 1 of the tree firmly planted by streams of water. The tree that yields abundant fruit. The tree whose leaves are perpetually green. This is the picture of a well-fed soul and a person who prospers in everything he or she does.

The psalm also tells us that such people delight in the Word of God. They keep good company (see #4: Choose Your Community Carefully). And they obey. So, certainly, Bible meditation and deep conversation and prayer should be a part of our spiritual diet.

> We CHECK GOD OFF OF OUR DAILY TO-DO LIST AND HARDLY THINK OF HIM AGAIN UNTIL OUR DESIGNATED BIBLE TIME TOMORROW.

Oh, here's the bit about "quiet times," you might be thinking. You might roll your eyes because you've heard it so many times before. Or you might skip over these paragraphs because you've got your "quiet times" sorted.

However, the way many of us think about our private devotional time is perhaps an outworking of modernist secularization—where there is a severe sacred and secular divide. Where we give God a focused half hour each morning and get it done, so we can move on with our life. We check Him off of our daily to-do list and hardly think of Him again until our designated Bible time tomorrow.

But what if our personal time in God's Word were to feed our soul in a more holistic way? What if that wasn't our only "time with God"? What if it made every minute of every day different? What if it helped us align our whole day with Him? What if it were our opportunity to enjoy a meal with our Maker that we then savored and found sustenance from for the rest of the day? This is what God intends.

He also offers us other foods to feed our soul, other ways to enjoy His presence. He provides other opportunities for us to grow, to be nourished and refreshed and attuned to Him.

In this chapter's Actions to Consider is a sample menu of what feeds us and a few of our friends. Order up an item or two. Cook up an idea of your own. Just don't wait any longer to create your own personalized meal plan. Work one or more of these into your week, and be better fed.

ACTIONS TO CONSIDER

Go for a long run or walk.

Share a meal with friends.

Meet with a small group.

Sing or listen to worship music.

Visit a museum.

Experience the liturgy.

Cuddle with your kids.

Play an instrument.

Paint, take photos, or create other art of your own.

Bake or cook.

Read a good book.

Purge and organize a closet.

Write in your journal.

Attend a conference or take a class.

QUESTIONS FOR REFLECTION AND DISCUSSION

- How are your eating habits?
- What improvements do you need to make to your eating habits? What measures of support and accountability can you put into place to ensure your success?
- What are you doing to feed your mind?
- What books do you want to read? What class could you take?
- What place do Bible meditation and conversation have in your spiritual diet? How might you add more of this?
- What other ways do you regularly feed your soul?

OTHER THINGS TO READ (AND WATCH)

Psalm 1

Philippians 3

Oswald Chambers, *My Utmost for His Highest: An Updated Edition in Today's Language* (Discovery House).

J. P. Moreland, *Love the Lord Your God with All Your Mind: The Role of Reason in the Life of the Soul* (NavPress).

A. W. Tozer, *The Pursuit of God: A Human Thirst for the Divine* (Moody).

The Danish movie *Babette's Feast*. The documentary *Super Size Me*.

#6

FOSTER
GOOD HABITS

As Annie Dillard said, "How we spend our days is, of course, how we spend our lives." So don't wait until tomorrow to get up early, go to bed on time, exercise enough, save money, and so on. The patterns of your life today are the person you will become.

> *All our life, so far as it has definite form,*
> *is but a mass of habits.*
>
> —WILLIAM JAMES

Yesterday was a Monday. And as I (Kelli) have done on most Mondays over the past two years, I printed out Daryl's "Responsibility Chart" and taped it onto one of our kitchen cupboard doors.

It's a deceptively simple chart. The columns are the days of the week, and the rows are the habits we are trying to encourage in our six-year-old son. Having his "God Time," exercising, doing his homework, clearing his dishes, picking up his toys, making his bed, practicing the piano, being kind to his three-year-old sister Amelia, and taking care of his brown and white guinea pig Sugar Cookie. Each time he completes a task, he puts a star in the appropriate box. Then, the number of stars on the chart at the end of the week affects the size of his allowance.

Unfortunately, though, actually cultivating these habits in Daryl's life is not as simple as our little chart system might lead one to believe. The first hurdle we regularly face is Daryl's resistance—surprise, surprise. He's human. He's a six-year-old boy. And he'd rather play with marbles or crash his cars than clean his room.

A second hurdle we face is time and the fact that some of our days look different from others. Some afternoons and evenings are wide open and free, and we have plenty of time to tick his chores off the list. Other days are crammed full of gymnastics lessons or errands or playdates with friends, making it hard to be as consistent as we'd like.

A third hurdle we face is me—surprise, surprise. I'm human too, and sometimes scatterbrained. On occasional Mondays I simply forget to print the chart out. Sometimes it's Thursday before I realize we have been freefalling for several days, and I do my best to reel us back in.

> GOOD HABITS TAKE EFFORT TO ESTABLISH AND MAINTAIN, BUT BAD HABITS HAPPEN EASILY—OFTEN WITHOUT ANY EFFORT AT ALL—AND THEY ARE HARD TO BREAK.

But in spite of these potential pitfalls and our own imperfections, we persist—because we know it's important. We've read the studies that say that children who develop good habits and discipline and self-control and willpower generally do better in life. We've also ex-perienced the reality that good habits take effort to establish and maintain, but bad habits happen easily—often without any effort at all—and they are hard to break.

HOW HABITS HAPPEN

What habits do you have right now?

If that question seems too vague, think through your daily routine.

When you woke up this morning, what did you do? Slap the snooze? Jump in the shower? Grab a bagel for breakfast? Make your bed? Walk your dog? Fill your travel mug with coffee?

On your way to work or school, did you adjust your rearview mirror? Turn on the radio? Take a shortcut to avoid traffic? Stop at a drive-thru? Slow down when you hit that speed trap?

Throughout your day, did you check your email or social media? Chew some gum? Make an online purchase? Drink a Diet Coke? Crack your knuckles? Get $20 out of a cash machine?

And when you got home, did you go for a run? Stick dinner in the microwave? Turn on the TV? Change your clothes? Do the dishes? Or sneak a midnight snack?

Regardless of whether your daily routine includes these spe-cific acts or others, the next question is this: Over which of these daily decisions did you actually deliberate?

Probably not many—if any.

Rather, in the course of your day, you performed these and many similar actions out of habit. One Duke University study discovered that over 40 percent of our behaviors are habitual.[1] Taken individually, each habit may not mean much. But when considered as a whole—as more than 40 percent of every day—our habits have a huge effect on our lives.

Over the past few decades, scientists have come to a deeper understanding of how habits happen. According to Charles Duhigg, each habit follows a predictable "three-step loop."[2]

First, there's a cue.[3] This might be a trigger, indicating a need. Or a signal, telling us something must be done. Or a prompt, letting us know that we should act.

Second, there's the routine.[4] This is the action we take in response to the cue. It's our attempt to meet the need or address the void.

Third, there's the reward.[5] This is the benefit we experience from the action we take. It's the reward that signals our brain that this loop is "worth remembering,"[6] and we should repeat this action—again. And again. And again.

Here are some examples of how this Habit Loop might work.

Our cue might be that every afternoon around two o'clock we feel sleepy. Our routine might be to find a cup of coffee—make a trip to the office coffee machine or, better yet, run over to the local coffee shop. Our reward, of course, is that we feel awake enough to finish our day.

Or our cue might be that every Monday morning we have a class or a meeting that we don't like. Our routine might be that we bite our fingernails through the whole thing. We systematically nibble those nails right down to the nub. And our reward may be that we feel calm enough or distracted enough to make it through all the Mondays.

Or our cue might be that our phone bings, indicating that we have a message or an email. Our routine may be to dig our phone out of our pocket or our purse so we can check it right away. Our reward is that our curiosity is satisfied and we feel connected and important—even when the message is nothing noteworthy.

Over time, this cue-routine-reward loop becomes more and more automatic. The cue and the reward become powerfully connected very deep in our brain until, eventually, the rest of our mind goes to sleep on the issue.[7] It stops consciously engaging with the behavior. The cue occurs. We perform the routine, and we receive the reward—all without a thought. And a habit is born.

CHANGING HABITS

Duhigg also identifies three additional elements that affect the Habit Loop. Craving[8] and belief[9] and community.[10]

Craving, of course, is the longing we develop for the reward we know we'll receive. Quite simply, we like the taste of chocolate, the buzz from caffeine, the endorphins when we run, the sense of satisfaction if we reach a new level on a computer game, and we want more. It's the craving that sets us in motion every time we experience the cue. It's the craving that drives us and blinds us and consumes us and makes our habits so powerful.

But even though they are powerful, "habits aren't destiny."[11] We need not feel defeated by our bad ones. They can be changed. Understanding the Habit Loop helps because, once we break it down into the individual parts, we can start fiddling with each bit.

New habits will reap new rewards of their own.

First, we can avoid a problematic cue or design a new one. We can take a different route to work if a particular drive-thru is too tempting. We can plan to exercise every evening as soon as we get home from work. We can change into our workout clothes as soon as we come in the door, so we give ourselves no opportunity to get distracted or deviate from the plan.

Second, we can replace an unhealthy routine with a healthy one. When we feel sleepy at 2:00 p.m., we can walk around the block instead of drinking a cup of caffeine. When we feel tempted" to shop, we can put some money into a savings account or give it to a charity instead of blowing it online.

Third, we can promise ourselves a new extrinsic reward for our efforts. We can plan to purchase a new outfit when we lose some weight. We can relax on a Friday and watch a movie after we've successfully kept our home clean all week. We can sleep in on Saturday when we've woken up early every other day for an early-morning prayer walk. But, too, these new habits will reap new rewards of their own. We will feel better physically. Our home will be a more peaceful refuge. Our hearts will be more in line with God's. And these new rewards will cultivate in us a new craving and, therefore, drive our new Habit Loop.

This is where belief comes in. The people who successfully design new cues and adopt healthy new routines and reap new rewards, the people who transform their bad habits into good are the people who believe that habits are important, that their life is of value, that change is possible, and that God gives the strength.

Finally, this belief is fostered in community. It happens best in the presence of prayer and encouragement and accountability and truth and love.

But here's the other key truth—the one that Duhigg didn't study. As followers of Jesus Christ, we are more than just creatures of habit. We are created beings, fashioned in the image of

God, and filled with the Holy Spirit. And it is in His power that we can be made new—habits and all.

A WORK IN PROGRESS

I (Kelli) am working on changing some of my habits—yet again—right now. Namely, I want to run every morning when I first get up, do Pilates every evening before I go to bed, eliminate caffeine from my daily diet, and eat less chocolate and sweets. I made my own "Responsibility Chart" of sorts, and I taped it to the inside of our medicine chest door. The chart itself acts as my cue. Every time I go for the toothpaste, I see it. My alarm clock is another cue, when it goes off each morning at four. Some mornings I still hit the snooze. But other mornings—more and more—I heed the cue and follow my desired routine. I roll out of bed, don my running shoes, and stumble down to the treadmill in the basement. Sure, I might mutter miserable complaints every step of the way. But when my run is finished each day, I feel better in every way. That is my reward.

Peter sees my chart too. He encourages me, reminds me, keeps me accountable. He is my community—even when I find it irritating, even when he finds me with my secret stash of milk chocolate chips and takes it away. He helps me believe—that my habits are important, that my life is of value, that change is possible, and that God gives me strength.

ACTIONS TO CONSIDER

Have a friend or family member tell you what habits they observe in your life—the good and the bad.

Respond differently to a common event (cue) in your life—your alarm going off, feeling drowsy in the afternoon, getting home from work. Develop a new routine. Establish a new reward.

QUESTIONS FOR REFLECTION AND DISCUSSION

- Did your parents instill any habits in you when you were a child? Did they stick? Why or why not?
- What habits do you have right now?
- Do you have any habits that you would like to change? If so, could you change the cue? How?
- Could you change the routine? What new routine might you try in its place?
- Could you motivate yourself with a new reward?
- What community could you count on to help you?

OTHER THINGS TO READ

Deuteronomy 6

Matthew 5–7

Charles Duhigg, *The Power of Habit: Why We Do What We Do in Life and Business* (Random House).

Donald S. Whitney, *Spiritual Disciplines for the Christian Life* (NavPress).

http://www.npr.org/2012/03/05/147192599/habits-how-they-form-and-how-to-break-them

#7

LEARN
TO REST

Though this could fall under "foster good habits," for me (Kelli) it deserves its own point. I am terrible at resting. I can trace this trouble back to my twenties—when I was single and lonesome and (more) insecure. To distract myself, I filled my days and nights to overflowing—a bit fuller and more frenetic each year. If I could, I would tell my twentysomething self that busy is not better, and your worth is not measured by the length of your to-do list.

Sometimes the most urgent and vital thing you
can possibly do is take a complete rest.

—Ashleigh Brilliant

I say that I can trace my overfull lifestyle and my lack of rest back to my twenties. But who am I kidding? It goes back way further than that. I can see it in the school-age little girl, who already felt lonesome and insecure much of the time. That little girl was often looking for more love than she sensed at home. She wanted to compensate for her perceived family deficiencies. She gave piano recitals and directed puppet shows and took ice skating lessons at the local rink. She soon realized that she received attention and praise for such activities and achievements—and got to liking it, craving it even.

It goes back to the high school girl who was even more hungry for acceptance and adoration. That young woman was even more embarrassed about all the ways she didn't fit in, so she entered speech competitions and writing competitions and auditioned for all the plays. She asked for lessons in flute and art and singing. She played volleyball and softball and cheered for the basketball team. She taught the children at church and got a job at fifteen. And over time she mistook admiration for true affection and became addicted to the adrenaline rush.

At twenty-two—right after college—I landed in the Chicago suburbs. I found myself alone in a one-bedroom apartment, with no family, no friends, and no activities. I had only a nine-to-five editing job on which to construct my adult identity, and I freaked.

It didn't take me long, though, to rebuild the busy. Graduate school. Gym memberships. Youth group ministry. And gradually, a social life. I refinished furniture, painted my apartment, and scheduled mission trips. Before I knew it, when anyone asked me, "How are you?" I could once again confidently respond, "Busy." I wore that "busy" like a badge. It became my trademark trait. Simultaneously, a plea for pity and a source of pride. It "worked" for me.

I know I'm not alone.

I know that many children today are involved in more activities than I ever dreamed of when I was their age. I know that many teens, too, feel the need to play sports and instruments, act in the plays, compete on the debate teams, and edit the school newspaper. They join the chess club and the art club and the before-school Bible study because participation in these things makes them "someone." I know that many young adults arrive

We lose control of our lives, and over time more and more activity is required to achieve the same "high."

at their twenties, and they add jobs and university courses and internships and ministry responsibilities and dating relationships to the mix. I know this because the college students—who collapse in the corner chair in my office every day and tell me they are "too busy"—confirm this conception: That many of us find too much of our worth in our full calendars.

However, busyness can happen for other reasons as well. In fact, a combination of contributing factors often causes the problem. We are also too busy because of our powerlessness to properly prioritize, our need to please other people, our fear of missing out on a good opportunity, or our addiction to productivity.

Busyness can become an addiction, make no mistake. It meets the criteria. We repeatedly engage in the "busy" *because* of the immediate rewards and *despite* the long-term and adverse consequences to our health, mental state, and relationships. We lose control of our lives, and over time more and more activity is required to achieve the same "high."

The book of Ecclesiastes addresses this vicious cycle— our chasing after pleasure and possessions, after wisdom and work, after money and the praise of people. It's all pointless, the Preacher says. Not because it's bad or wrong in and of itself. But because we were made for so much more. He has set eternity in our hearts.

This is why we need to nip busyness in the bud.

This is why we need to learn to rest.

CREATED FOR REST

It isn't a new notion, rest. It isn't a twenty-first-century need. God doesn't mandate rest in response to our modern-day mayhem. No.

Rather, it goes all the way back to The World—Week One. God built rest right into His creation. It's central to His design. For six days, He worked. He made day and night. The land and the seas. The plants and the animals and the people in His image. And with each new construction, He stopped and He looked and He saw and He said, "It is good."

Then, on the seventh day, He rested. He took a Sabbath and sanctified it.

Our lives still operate on His seven-day cycle. For six days we work, and every seventh day we are called to rest—to take a Sabbath and sanctify it. It's built right into our DNA.

Rest encourages reflection, so we can move more mindfully through life. Rest replenishes a tired body, so we can reengage with strength. Rest refocuses our soul on the things of God. Rest is an essential element of a life rightly lived. We need rest like we need water and air.

A CURE FOR RESTLESSNESS

The irony behind this chapter is that—while we are writing it—our lives are perhaps busier than ever before. We are both professors—designing lessons, grading papers, attending meetings, mentoring students. We host a small group for our church, and I run a writing workshop for some wonderful women. We have two active children. And admittedly, at ages six and three, they have already taken violin lessons and swim lessons and gymnastics classes—though by conviction we have recently cut back. Peter and I both accept additional speaking engagements, we love building into our friendships, we work to make our marriage a priority, and now we are writing a book.

So yes, I feel a bit of a fraud.

But here's the thing. Though I don't write about rest as someone who steadily succeeds in this area, I do write as someone who has suffered regularly the results of getting it wrong. Growth on this point has been slow. Addiction is hard to overcome. But thankfully, God is patient as He works to reshape my image of myself. He gradually grounds my identity in His Son alone. He continually clarifies His call on my life. He communicates what He wants me to let in and what He wants me to leave out. And thankfully, He persistently pierces my present, helping me to stop, to see what He has given, and to proclaim with Him that "It is good." And it is enough.

ACCEPT ONLY THOSE ASSIGNMENTS THAT HE HAS CLEARLY CALLED US TO, AND DECLINE INVITATIONS WHEN NECESSARY AND WITHOUT SHAME.

By the grace of God, then, I no longer wear that "busy" as a badge. It's no longer a virtue or a goal in my eyes. I no longer tell people "I'm busy," looking for pity or puffing with pride. I instead ask for prayer and wisdom and strength. I pray for open ears and open eyes. And I work to reclaim my rest.

Doing this is not necessarily as simple as it sounds—at least it hasn't been for me. We must start with a change of heart, a change of focus. A first important cure for the overly busy life is to foster a secure identity that doesn't depend on what we do. We must remind ourselves daily—hourly—that who we are hinges only on who *God* is and what *He* has done. Our feeble efforts to add value are empty. See Ecclesiastes.

A second cure is to listen carefully, to let into our lives only those commitments that God gives us license to allow. Accept only those assignments that He has clearly called us to, and decline invitations when necessary and without shame. Remember that every yes we utter necessitates another no. If we take on something new, of what are we willing to let go?

A third cure is to foster a proper appreciation for the present. We must cultivate contentment. Daily—hourly—stop and look and see what He has given. We ought to say to ourselves and bear witness to others that "It is good." When we fully appreciate what *is*, we feel less compelled to add more.

A fourth cure is to establish a Sabbath—whether it's Saturday or Sunday or some other space we can create in our schedule. Set that time in stone. Shield it. Savor it. It is sanctified.

HOW WE'RE LEARNING TO REST

Our wedding anniversary is December 18.

This is probably the worst possible time of year for such a significant celebration to occur. We chose that date for reasons that made sense fifteen years ago. Namely, we had to get married during a school break and we didn't want to wait until the following summer. But every year since then we have found it difficult to just drop everything and commemorate our relationship.

This year was no different.

Around December 15 we were both up to our necks in grading. We had barely begun to prepare for Christmas. We were falling behind on our book project. And the subject came up— what should we do for our anniversary?

I'm sure Peter saw my tired eyes and felt my exhaustion just before he picked up his phone and took matters into his own hands. Since money was also a concern, he called a friend who works at a nearby camp. He was able to get us a room at their conference center, overlooking the lovely Lake Geneva. Peter's mum agreed to take the kids, and that Thursday we got away.

For a few hours that evening, in an attempt to unwind, we wandered the quiet streets and perused the quirky shops of that lakeside town. We savored a slow seafood dinner. We slept for ten hours straight—longer than either of us can remember sleeping for years. We had plenty of time to talk, to really see each other again. And it was good.

The next morning we had breakfast at the eccentric Daddy Maxwell's Antarctic Circle Diner—the one shaped like an igloo and decorated in a kitschy 1950s style. Peter had their special French batter pancakes, and I had an omelet. We ate slowly— uninterrupted—and enjoyed every bite.

Then we took our time driving home—reconnected and refreshed—and reminded, once again, of why it is crucial for all of us to rest.

ACTIONS TO CONSIDER

Clear your schedule and take a weekend away—by yourself or with friends. Have no agenda other than rest.

If you are overcommitted, be ruthless in cutting one thing out of your life.

In the middle of the day, take one hour to sit in a room and do *nothing*. Discuss with a friend what happened.

QUESTIONS FOR REFLECTION AND DISCUSSION

- Is your life too busy right now?
- If you answered yes, do you know why you have filled it so full? Do any of the possible reasons given in this chapter resonate with you?
- What place does rest have in your life?
- How might you live more purposefully in the *present*?
- Do you keep a Sabbath? If yes, how does it affect the rest of your life? If no, how could you add a Sabbath to your weekly schedule?

OTHER THINGS TO READ

Genesis 1 and 2

Ecclesiastes

Mark 6

Henry Cloud and John Townsend, *Boundaries: When to Say Yes, How to Say No to Take Control of Your Life* (Zondervan).

www.chattingatthesky.com

#8

BE
PATIENT

Learn to wait well. You are used to getting things in an instant and on demand, but life doesn't always work that way. Neither does God. His timing is rarely yours, but His is always right. He doesn't rush, and He never delays. Instead, He unfolds a plan carefully designed and perfectly timed to bring Him glory.

"Wait on the Lord" is a constant refrain in the Psalms, and it is a necessary word, for God often keeps us waiting. He is not in such a hurry as we are, and it is not his way to give more light on the future than we need for action in the present, or to guide us more than one step at a time. When in doubt, do nothing, but continue to wait on God. When action is needed, light will come.

—J. I. PACKER, *KNOWING GOD*

Last spring the Hidden Pearl coffee shop opened in downtown McHenry—just two blocks south of our house on Green Street. It changed our lives and our hopes for the neighborhood, which has endured its share of fallout from the latest economic downturn.

It lives up to its name, this Hidden Pearl. It's hard to spot—even though it sits on one of the busiest streets through town, between the now-abandoned movie theater and a new tattoo parlor. The exterior is brown and bland, and the signage subtle. White chalk on a blackboard in the window. Almost every time I (Kelli) am in there, I overhear another new customer ask the owner, "How long have you been here?" When he says, "Six months," or seven or eight, the typical reply is, "I had no idea." The tone is usually a mix of both shame and delight. Shame at not discovering the place sooner. And delight, because it only takes a moment for new patrons to recognize the other truth . . .

That the Hidden Pearl is also precious—a rare gem in our struggling town. The coffee is rich. The baked goods are delectable. And don't get me started on the ham, egg, and cheese croissant—with just the right amount of fresh cracked pepper. The staff is kind, and they know you by name. But it is perhaps the décor that I love the most: the attention to detail and beauty, the latte-and-chocolate-colored walls, the turquoise Victorian couch and pillows and vases on the shelves, the vintage posters of Paris, the leafy palm. The Hidden Pearl is an oasis, defying the busyness of life and inviting you to linger.

One afternoon Peter and I were doing just that. We were sitting on the sofa, catching up over coffee. Daryl and Amelia were sharing a cookie. Several

One OF THE HARDEST THINGS YOU COULD EVER ASK US TO DO IS WAIT.

other customers were sipping drinks and savoring baked goods, and there was the pleasant buzz of conversation.

Then a woman came in.

I didn't hear her order, and I didn't notice her waiting—until suddenly, out of the corner of my eye, I saw her stand up, say something spiteful to the owner, and storm out. I saw the startled look on the owner's face. Then I saw him hurry out the back door of the shop, letting the door slam behind.

Sometime later he reappeared, still shaken.

When he came to clear our cups, we tried to console him with compliments about the chocolate cake. Then Peter asked him—straight up—if everything was okay.

"She doesn't get who we are," the owner said.

And we agreed. "If she just wants her coffee fast," I said, "there are plenty of other places to go in town." We shook our heads in disbelief.

That afternoon the same woman took her outrage to the Internet, posting a scathing review on the Hidden Pearl Facebook page. She called the service poor and the wait ridiculous. And how could they even call themselves a coffee shop when it took them so long to make a cup?

When I saw that woman, certainly I saw our society. But—to be perfectly honest—I also saw myself.

A PEOPLE ON THE GO

I don't have to tell you that we are a people on the go. With our fast food and our express checkout and our ability to have just about anything delivered to our doorstep—tomorrow—if we are so inclined. We invest much time and money into figuring out how to make things move more quickly. From our transportation, to our technology. From our education, to our work. From our health, to our finances, to our relationships, and even to our worship.

We value speed over safety. Efficiency over integrity. Convenience over quality. Immediate profitability over patience. And one of the hardest things you could ever ask us to do is wait.

Innumerable fascinating studies have been done to try to quantify our obsession with speed. Last year computer science professor Ramesh Sitaraman examined the viewing habits of 6.7 million Internet users below the age of thirty-five. He monitored how long people are willing to wait for a video to load on the web.

Two seconds, he found.

After that, we start abandoning. "After five seconds, the abandonment rate is 25 percent," he marveled. "When you get to ten seconds, more than half are gone."[1]

In a 2013 experiment, Frank May and Ashwani Monga tried to determine what factors influenced people's willingness to wait. In one study, they offered grocery shoppers the option of a $5 gift certificate today or a $10 gift certificate that wasn't valid until next week. They found that people's choice between less/now or more/later was, in part, connected to their perception of their own power. Interestingly, people who had a greater sense of power tended to exhibit more patience and pick the later prize.[2]

In a companion study, May and Monga monitored university students' selection of either standard shipping or expedited when they purchased a pair of sunglasses online. Then they asked each student—straight up—how he or she viewed time. As a negative force working against them or a positive force that was on their side? As a source of pain or pleasure? As good or bad?[3]

As you may imagine, time has a significant image problem.

A CUSTOMIZED LIFE

But time is not the only trouble.

In his article "Instant Gratification" in the *American Scholar* journal, Paul Roberts makes another—related—observation. Not only are we a culture that wants things in a hurry, but we also want them in a very particular way. We expect our own desires to be met on demand. He describes our consumer culture as "almost too good at giving us what we want."[4]

Here he explains: "I don't just mean the way smartphones and search engines and Netflix and Amazon anticipate our preferences. I mean how the entire edifice of the consumer economy, digital and actual, has reoriented itself around our own agendas, self-images, and inner fantasies. . . . It is now entirely normal to demand a personally customized life. We fine-tune our moods with pharmaceuticals and Spotify. We craft our meals around our allergies and ideologies. We can choose a vehicle to express our hipness or hostility. We can move to a neighborhood that matches our social values, find a news outlet that mirrors our politics, and create a social network that 'likes' everything we say or post. With each transaction and upgrade, each choice and click, life moves closer to us, and the world becomes our world."[5]

And so, we live at a time and in a place that affords us an unnatural and unhealthy level of control. But it is pseudocontrol. And we are pseudogods. Revving our pitiful engines. Pressing our feet hard on the pedal. Racing around and around. Chasing after the wind. Forgetting the fact that obtaining our pseudoprize isn't even the point.

WHEN WE WAIT

I (Kelli) have had several prolonged periods of waiting in my life. In my twenties, I waited several years for a much-desired career change. I waited even longer to start a second graduate program. And I waited that whole long decade to marry, not meeting Peter until I was months from thirty.

That wait to be married was certainly the most difficult wait for me because it required far more than patience to endure. It often demanded a strength and a faith beyond my own ready reserves. A strength to make a life for myself—all by myself—in a great big new city. And a faith to believe that God did, indeed, have my good in mind. Because on a regular basis I found myself in situations that seemed to highlight my solo status and the ache in my heart. When a new friend and I visited the singles groups at several area churches, looking for fun and friends, we found at these gatherings either a meat market or a mopey support group. And admittedly, we slipped out early—frustrated and confused.

When I tried the adult Sunday school class at my new church and found it full of couples, talking about couple-ish things, I quickly volunteered to teach the Sunday school class for the junior high girls—in part, because I wanted to serve and I cared about the youth. But admittedly, I didn't feel as if I fit anywhere else. When a dating relationship ended just before Christmas and I spent a quiet New Year's Eve alone in my apartment, I determined to devote that evening to goal setting with God.

> Year after year he weaves waiting into the very fabric of our lives. We wait for all sorts of things, and we rarely like it.

But admittedly, the rejection poked holes in my identity that took months (years?) to repair. And every time I donned a poofy dress and sauntered down a church aisle and stood smiling off to the side while another friend pledged her love and her life, I *was* happy for that bride. But admittedly, at the same time, I battled jealousy and fear. Why not me? Would it ever be?

Sometimes when I got impatient with the delay, I took matters into my own hands. I forced the issue of marriage with my boyfriend at the time, or I gave too much of myself too soon to someone I barely knew. Those were some of the destructive ways I sought to bring the wait to a premature end. I watched other friends resolve the same sense of urgency by marrying quickly— while the infatuation still burned hot—and I watched too many of those marriages end—some sooner, some later—in painful divorce. Then I saw still other people try to fill the void with various, unsatisfactory things: excessive activity, purchases, substances.

THE INVITATION

The more I've seen and heard, however, and the more waiting I've done myself, the more it's been confirmed to me that waiting is central to the human experience, that God ordained this to be, and that year after year He weaves waiting into the very fabric of our lives. We wait for the next event or for the end to a particular pain. We wait for clarity and for answers to prayer. We wait for all sorts of things, and we rarely like it.

But I've also seen that waiting has its place. It causes us to slow down and refocus and number the days. It is meant to be a time of preparation and anticipation and dependence on Him, and we learn things while we wait that we would never otherwise know. Jerome Daley calls the waiting room "an invitation to intimacy."[6] And I believe he's right.

In his book *When God Waits,* Daley also lists many people in God's Word who spent a surprisingly long time in the waiting room of life. Abraham (25 years). Joseph (13 and more). Moses (40 years, then 40 years again). Hannah (5 to 15 years). To name just a few.

This year, though, my favorite biblical passage on waiting has been John chapter 11. It's the famous story of Jesus raising Lazarus from the dead. You probably already know the climax of the story, where Jesus calls into the cave and "the dead man came out."

But there is a lot of important story before that point.

In the opening verses of the chapter, we learn that Lazarus is ill and that his sisters send for Jesus, saying, "The one you love is ill." Then in verses 4 and 6, John makes it clear that Jesus receives the message. I love that John tells us this twice, that he makes sure we know—"Jesus heard."

He always hears. Even when we think He hasn't, He hears.

But He doesn't always hurry, and He certainly doesn't in Lazarus's case.

For two crucial days, the passage tells us, Jesus stays put. He doesn't rush to the scene. He lets Lazarus rest in peace while Mary and Martha and the other mourners grieve and wail and wonder why He does not come.

The Jews of the time believed that the soul of a dead person remained in the vicinity of the body for three days, hoping to reenter it. But once decomposition set in, the soul departed. In part, then, Jesus waits so that the dramatic resurrection He has planned cannot be misconstrued as a simple resuscitation.

Jesus' goal with this impending miracle is the glory of God.

We know this because He says so. He tells His disciples. Twice. "This illness does not lead to death. It is for the glory of God" (John 11:4). And lest we miss the point, He repeats this truth a third time at the tomb.

Then, too—though the glory of God could certainly be an end in itself—Jesus clearly states that there is another purpose as well. God's glory will be on full display so that the people will believe. He repeats that point too. And in verses 41–42, He prefaces the miracle with a public prayer. "Father, I thank you that you have heard me. I knew that you always hear me, but I said this on account of the people standing around, that they may believe that you sent me."

Then, in that climactic and wondrous event, He shouts into the dark tomb and calls forth life. Sure enough, many believe. The divine delay results in a display of God's glory, which leads to belief.

SOME WAYS WE CAN WAIT WELL

So the question then becomes—not *will* we have to wait or *why*. The question that remains is "*how*." When we find ourselves lined up along the wall, twiddling our thumbs, what can we do? Here are five ideas:

Look around. When we are in the waiting room, we tend to fix our eyes on the exit sign. We keep listening for our name to be called, so we can get out of there and move on to what really matters. We long so much for a future ideal that we forget to value and fully engage with our present reality—the floor right beneath our feet. But we can't live in the future—or the past, for that matter. We can only live today. This moment. So we do well—even as we wait—to open our eyes to what is right in front of us. We do well to love the people across the room and give ourselves fully to whatever God has given us to do right now.

Get ready. The waiting room need not be a stagnant space. In fact, it can be a time of great growth. A greenhouse of sorts—if you'll pardon the mixing of the metaphors. It can be an opportunity to deepen our roots before we are called upon to spread our limbs and produce fruit. Or maybe it's more like a weight room—a place to build up our muscle mass before the big game. Regardless of which image holds appeal, we must make full use of the time. We should train thoroughly. Go to school. Take a class. Read good books. Sharpen our skills. Cultivate character. Gain experience. Volunteer our time. Refine our relational skills. Meet with a counselor. Build a network. Assemble resources. Set some goals. Make a plan and follow through and practice prayer. So when our name is called, we are all ready to go.

Find the fun. Admittedly, life in the waiting room can be drab and difficult. The walls are grey. The chairs, uncomfortable. The magazines are outdated, and who actually reads *Golf Digest* anyhow? But we know that "Life is 10 percent what happens to you and 90 percent how you respond to it." And though it sounds cliché, we know that it often rings true. So rather than resigning ourselves to the negative emotions, rather than assuming we will only be happy when we bust out of this place, we can seek enjoyment right in the midst. When I was in my twenties, this looked like backpacking trips and cooking

> GOD NOT ONLY CREATED THE WAITING ROOM, HE INHABITS IT. IT IS ACTUALLY THE SITE OF SOME OF HIS MOST PROFOUND WORK.

classes and long coffee dates and a spontaneous skydiving adventure that I will never forget.

Foster hope. It's easy for hope to fade when the wait drags on—when we hear everyone else's name called but ours—when we begin to wonder if the receptionist even remembers that we're sitting there, playing Solitaire on our phone. Truthfully, some of us find that it's easier not to hope at all, so we stuff our dreams into the bottom of our bag and try to forget that they even exist. Maybe that's because the object of our "hope" is our own desires. We hope in this sense: "I hope I get what I want." And truthfully, this sort of hope is fragile. This sort of hope will surge and recede with every change of circumstance. There are no guarantees. Yet, still, we must believe. It's the object of our hope that may need to change. Our hope must be placed in something certain and sure. That is, God Himself. His presence. His power. His glory. And eternity as He has designed.

Draw close. When we feel stuck in the waiting room—and the days turn into months and the months turn into years—we may imagine that God is off somewhere behind closed doors, giving all of His time and attention to someone else. However, He not only created the waiting room, He inhabits it. It is actually the site of some of His most profound work. So let's climb up next to Him. Let's draw close and listen carefully to whatever He wants to whisper in our ear.

ACTIONS TO CONSIDER

While waiting in a line or a waiting room somewhere, ask yourself how you feel. How can this time be used for good? Who else can you reach out to in that moment?

Think about what you would miss if you were able to fast-forward to an event you are waiting for.

Draw out your ideal timeline for your life. Release this to God in prayer.

QUESTIONS FOR REFLECTION AND DISCUSSION

- How was waiting modeled for you by your parents? By your culture?
- What are you waiting for right now?
- Describe your thoughts, feelings, and actions while you wait.
- How do you think a person can wait well?
- What have you seen God do in the waiting room—in your life and the lives of others?

OTHER THINGS TO READ

Psalms 27 and 40

John 11

Jerome Daley, *When God Waits: Making Sense of Divine Delays* (WaterBrook).

Jeff Goins, *The In-Between: Embracing the Tension between Now and the Next Big Thing* (Moody).

David Timms, *Sacred Waiting: Waiting on God in a World That Waits for Nothing* (Bethany).

#9

DON'T
WORRY

It's a waste of time, energy, and emotion. Worry will tie you in knots. Keep you up at night. Make you cranky and crazy. Nothing good ever comes of it. Worry is fear for the future, but worry does nothing to actually change it. So instead of worrying, make the best decisions you can right now. That's all you can do. Then let it be.

Worry does not empty tomorrow of its sorrow;
it empties today of its strength.

—CORRIE TEN BOOM, *CLIPPINGS FROM MY NOTEBOOK*

Our six-year-old son Daryl couldn't sleep last night. He tossed and turned for some time. Then he turned on his light and read a few books. Eventually, we could hear him jumping on his bed and riding his skateboard up and down our long upstairs hallway. That's when it was time to intervene. After Peter confiscated the skateboard, we had a little chat. I (Kelli) asked him if something was wrong, but he couldn't say. So we prayed together. I gave him a few more cuddles and turned on some music. Then I tucked him in and left him to rest again, quietly on his own. Before long, though, he appeared one more time at the bottom of the stairs.

"I keep seeing scary things in my mind," he said, but he couldn't nail it down much more than that. Once again I took him by the hand and led him back to bed.

While Peter tends to take a no-nonsense approach when the kids have sleeping troubles, I have perhaps too much empathy for Daryl's occasional late-night fears. As a kid, I spent many sleepless nights worrying. Every time my parents left me with a babysitter, I sat by the window, staring at the driveway and crying copious tears, convinced that every police car screaming by was racing to their demise. Because of my parents' cerebral palsy and physical limitations, because my dad often fell down and my mom was often overwhelmed, I was never fully convinced that they could take care of themselves, let alone my brother and me. Then, occasional incidents—such as the following—confirmed my fears and my belief that the safety of our entire family depended on me . . .

One February night when I was ten, I woke up to my mom's shout. "Kelli! There's a fire!" My brother, then age seven, had been sleeping alone in his big upstairs room. He came down in the middle of the night to find my parents and tell them that he was hot. My mom smelled the smoke.

I don't remember if my parents told me to investigate or if I decided to do so of my own accord. Probably the latter, but whatever the case, while my mom called the fire department and my dad ushered my brother out of the house, I filled my lungs with clean air and ran up the stairs. The entire space was full of smoke. I opened a window and ran back down the stairs to take a breath. Then I made another trip to find the source. Through the haze, I could just barely make it out. In the center of my brother's twin mattress was a big, black, smoldering spot. I grabbed the mattress and pulled. With great effort, by the time the fire engines arrived, I had dragged the mattress through the house and out to the street.

The local newspaper ran an article about the dangers of old electric blankets—the cause of our fire. The reporter mentioned my parents by name and my little brother and even his stuffed dog, which suffered terrible burns. But the article didn't mention me—the self-proclaimed savior of the story. Yes, I was miffed about the lack of public praise for my heroic act, but this Great Mattress Fire of 1980 also solidified my tendency toward anxiety.

WHEN WORRY GOES UNCHECKED

Left unaddressed, my childhood worry turned into full-blown, grown-up worry in my twenties. I worried about finding a job, finding an apartment, finding a husband, paying my bills. I worried about getting into a graduate program, and when I got into one, I worried about not doing well. I still worried about my family from afar. And I also worried about my friends and my church and my youth group mentees and what in the world I was going to do with the rest of my life.

Then, in my early thirties, I suddenly had more to worry about than ever before. Peter and I bought our 1920s Craftsman home in McHenry, Illinois—with my parents—and we planned to move them down from Minnesota to live with us. When we signed the contract, my mom and dad were both in relatively good health—in spite of their disabilities—so we anticipated living together for a good long time. My plan was to resign from my teaching job so I could stay at home, caring for our children and my parents. But God had other ideas.

Before my parents could even make the move, my mom was diagnosed with cancer. She started her chemo in Minneapolis, and then they moved to McHenry a few months later. She had surgery and more treatment, and eventually— for a few months—she felt pretty good, and we all caught our breath.

On many mornings I would bolt awake at 3:15 a.m. and my first instinct was to worry.

Then my dad fell and broke his hip, and Mom's cancer returned. Because of my dad's costly nursing home care, our whole financial forecast looked bleak, and we feared we would lose the house. In the midst of this, Peter and I suffered multiple miscarriages and endured delayed and disrupted adoptions—and our marriage was showing the strain of it all.

During this time, on many mornings I would bolt awake at 3:15 a.m. and my first instinct was to worry. As soon as I opened my eyes and glanced at the clock, my mind would begin to whir. What if Mom dies? What if I can't care for Dad and we can't bring him back home? What if we have to sell our house? What if we never have a child? What if Peter finds this all too much? What if? What if? What if?

Not wanting to wake Peter with my tossing and turning, I would slip downstairs to the sofa. I would lie there in the dark; sometimes I would read books. Sometimes my Bible. Sometimes I would journal, and my desperate, scribbled words would usually become a prayer. Not an eloquent one, by any means. Something more akin to "Help."

By the grace of God, He did.

He didn't heal my mom or my dad. My mom passed away. We were never able to bring my dad back home, and he died eighteen months after Mom. Peter and I never had a successful pregnancy. While we managed to keep the house, a whole lot of money was lost. The difficult things still happened. Some of the very painful problems I worried about did come about.

However, God did something even greater than giving me all of my affirmative answers to prayer. He gave me Himself. And for many mornings at 3:15 a.m. that sofa became a sanctuary, a place for Him to do His good work.

JESUS ON WORRY

When Jesus taught His disciples about the kingdom of God in the Sermon on the Mount, He told them, "Do not be anxious about your life" (Matthew 6:25). When Paul wrote to the struggling church in Philippi, he told them, "Do not be anxious about anything" (Philippians 4:6). When Peter wrote to God's scattered people, he told them to cast "all your anxieties on him, because he cares for you" (1 Peter 5:7).

Initially, when I (Peter) read this advice, it actually irritated me. It sounded as if I just need to get over my worry. Just stop being anxious already. It reminded me of my father's unhelpful admonition: "Pull yourself together, boy!" The Bible, too, can seem unhelpful at times—until we look at its counsel in context.

In His Sermon on the Mount, Jesus addresses His words on worry to people who are concerned about basic material needs.

WORRY IS UNIVERSAL, AND IT IS AS COMPLEX AND DIVERSE AND RELENTLESS AS WE ARE. JESUS KNEW THAT.

They have questions of simple survival. "What shall I eat? What shall I drink? What shall I wear?" For His initial audience, these were quite possibly their primary problems. Certainly and sadly, for hundreds of millions of people around the world today, this is still the case. In the United States alone, 14.9 percent of households spent at least part of the year (2011) living "food insecure." Of those, 5.7 percent experienced "very low food security."[1] Maybe you can relate. Maybe these are your worries as well. Maybe they are the worries of people you love.

Many of us, though, *do* have enough food to eat and clean water to drink. We have plenty of clothes to wear, but we still worry all the same—we just worry about different things. Worry is universal, and it is as complex and diverse and relentless as we are. Jesus knew that.

That's why He doesn't just tell us to "get over it." He doesn't just say, "Don't be anxious." Period. End of discussion. No. Instead, He spends some time on the topic. He gives His audience—and us—a powerful and multifaceted antidote for anxiety.

First of all, Jesus surrounds His "don't worry about your life" message with beautiful imagery of nature. He tells His audience to look at the birds, flying freely overhead. They don't do any work in the field, Jesus observes. They don't sow or reap or gather grain into barns. Yet they have plenty to eat—because they are fed by God. Then He asks His listeners to concentrate on a flower. Traditionally, it's been called a lily of the field. Can you picture it? That lily—with its intricately painted petals, kissed by the sun. With its long, graceful stem, waving in a warm summer breeze.

That lily doesn't work, Jesus reminds us. That lily doesn't make its own clothes. It's not up to the lily what it wears. God cares for it. Then, Jesus says, how much more will He care for you, crown of His creation? So the first step in releasing our worry—Jesus' way—is to realize and remember our value to Him. He knows your needs, Jesus says, so trust the One who treasures you.

Second, it is difficult to release one behavior without replacing it with another. It is difficult, if not impossible, to let go of worry without refocusing and retraining the mind toward something else. Jesus tells His listeners—and us—quite plainly what that new object of our attention ought to be. He says, "Seek first the kingdom of God and his righteousness" (Matthew 6:33). In other words, the second step in moving beyond our worry is to set our sights on the things of God. Actively pursue Him and actively pursue Christlikeness—above all else. Above food and water and clothing. Above jobs and apartments and spouses. Above safety and comfort and control. And as you do, Jesus says, God will give you just what you need.

Third, we must understand that worry lives in the future. It draws our focus to all of the possible *what ifs*, which seriously inhibits our ability to deal well with *what is*. Jesus knew this too, of course. He finishes His words on worry with another challenge. "Therefore do not be anxious about tomorrow, for tomorrow will be anxious for itself" (Matthew 6:34). Instead of spending our mental and emotional energy wondering what will come, we must decide to live in the here and now. We must be present and grateful for what God has given us today. And we must look to Him for the strength to handle it.

PAUL ON WORRY

The apostle Paul undoubtedly knew Jesus' teaching on worry, but in his letter to the Philippian church—a group of people who had plenty of their own reasons to fret—Paul gives his own spin on how to live a worry-free life. Remember, he's writing from a Roman prison, so he ought to know a thing or two.

"Do not be anxious about anything," Paul writes (Philippians 4:6). It's another simple and direct command. But it's in the surrounding verses that Paul tells the Philippians—and us—more about the *hows* and the *whys*.

Worry-free living starts with an intentional and continual expression of joy. "Rejoice in the Lord always," Paul says. "Again I will say, Rejoice" (Philippians 4:4). But it sounds unrealistic, doesn't it? It sounds like an ancient version of the song "Don't Worry, Be Happy"—as if it were that simple, as if we can just flip a switch, as if we can feel joyful on demand. Perhaps it helps to notice that this joy is an action, rather than an attitude. It's something we can *do* even when the obstacles of life threaten to overwhelm. Even when we start to *feel* anxious and afraid, we can rejoice—because the object is not our circumstances. The object is our God, who never changes, who always cares, and who is always near.

GIVE YOUR CONCERNS TO HIM—WITH GRATITUDE. OVER AND OVER AND OVER AGAIN.

Next, Paul says that the alternative to worry is prayer and the antidote to anxiety is thanksgiving. "Let your requests be made known to God," he declares (Philippians 4:6). Give your concerns to Him—with gratitude. Not once. Not twice. But over and over and over again. Every time a worry crops up, every time your chest tightens and you find it hard to breathe, every time you wake up at 3:15 a.m. and sneak down to the sofa, every time you see scary things in your mind—lay them at His feet, saying, "Here, God. Thank You. And help."

Finally, Paul promises, the peace of God—which transcends all understanding—*will* gradually break through.

ACTIONS TO CONSIDER

Sit in the presence of God and be honest about your anxiety and worry. Let yourself feel it.

Look at nature and contemplate how God cares for you.

Repeatedly give your anxiety and worries to God.

Think on what is noble, pure, and lovely.

QUESTIONS FOR REFLECTION AND DISCUSSION

- How often do you worry? Is worry a chronic problem for you? Or just an occasional event?
- How does worry affect your life?
- Was worry a part of your childhood experience? If so, why? What did you worry about then?
- Which part of Jesus' Sermon on the Mount section on worry speaks to you the most?
- Which part of Philippians 4 resonates with you?
- What will you do differently the next time worry threatens to take over your mind?

OTHER THINGS TO READ

Matthew 6

Philippians 4

Archibald Hart, *The Anxiety Cure: A Proven Method for Dealing with Worry, Stress, and Panic Attacks* (Thomas Nelson).

Ray Kane and Nancy Kane, *From Fear to Love: Overcoming the Barriers to Healthy Relationships* (Moody).

#10

ADJUST YOUR EXPECTATIONS

So much of our disappointment and frustration—with people, with life, with God—occurs because we presume that life should go *our* way. I (Kelli) still remember the Friday night when the lightbulb of this lesson first switched on for me. Years ago I was driving home from work, mulling over my expectations for the weekend and already becoming irritated, knowing that they wouldn't be met. So I decided to change them. I made the conscious decision to rewrite my personal plan for those two days. I put only one thing on my new agenda: "Love Peter well." *That* I could do. Over Peter himself I had no control, but I did have control over my own mind. Lo and behold, our weekend went well, and I was in no way disappointed.

The sun'll come out tomorrow,
Bet your bottom dollar that
tomorrow there'll be sun.

—ANNIE

"Eeyore," said Owl, "Christo-
pher Robin is giving a party."
"Very interesting," said Eeyore.
"I suppose they will be sending
me down the odd bits which
got trodden on."

—A.A. MILNE, *WINNIE THE POOH*

My birthday has been a complicated affair ever since I (Peter) was six.

That year my mum planned a party. She decorated the house with balloons, filled bowls with jelly (Jell-O) and ice cream, made a hedgehog cake out of chocolate buttons, and invited many of my school and neighborhood friends. She planned several party games and prepared a prize for the winner of each. Like most six-year-olds, I was perhaps most excited about the possibility of presents.

But.

On the day of the party, no one came. Not one.

That year my birthday fell on Easter weekend, and every last friend had gone out of town. They didn't call. They didn't send their regrets. They just didn't show up.

"They'll be here any minute," my mum kept reassuring me, but the doorbell never rang. She, my dad, and my grandmother tried their best to carry on. They played party game after party game with me, and they laughed and cheered with extra exuberance to fill the void. We eventually cut the cake and ate the ice cream. But I was devastated. And—believe it or not—

I don't think I have ever fully recovered from my six-year-old disappointment.

I (Kelli) have heard Peter's forlorn six-year-old birthday party story many, many times in our fifteen years as husband and wife. It inevitably comes up every year around his birthday—and almost any time we plan a party or a gathering of friends. Ironically, Peter loves hosting events. He regularly throws game nights and invites dozens of friends each time. But often, as party day approaches, he vacillates between Annie-like anticipation and Eeyore-esque resignation to doom because deep down six-year-old Peter is convinced that no one will come.

The mental image of my husband as a six-year-old, staring at his hedgehog cake and waiting for the doorbell to ring, breaks my heart every time he talks about it. So you would think that I would take great care to make his birthday celebration special each year.

Certainly, some years I have. For his thirtieth birthday—his first birthday after our marriage—I surprised him with not one, but three, parties because our tiny apartment could only accommodate four guests at a time. I ordered a bright blue Thomas the Tank Engine cake, reminiscent of the one he himself had requested as a joke when he was seventeen. That thirtieth year he seemed to enjoy the gag and the three birthday gatherings and the fact that his new wife loved him so well. I met his expectations, and then some.

However.

On the day of his thirty-eighth birthday, I failed.

That year Peter's birthday fell on a Wednesday, a day when both of us had to work. It also fell on an evening when I was required to attend a book reading for graduate school. I don't know exactly what he expected to happen that night. My plan was to wait and celebrate with him on the weekend, so I thought I still had a few days to purchase presents and make a plan. Still, rather than be away from Peter on his actual birthday, I did what any thoughtful wife would do. I invited him to come along to my school. Begrudgingly, he did. But it was bad. The reading was a bore. Peter felt ignored. We argued the whole way home. In the end, Peter went to bed early, while I ran over to a local shop to buy a balloon and a card and some subpar, spur-of-the-moment gifts to make amends.

UNMET EXPECTATIONS

Expectations happen to all of us.

Often they crop up—unconsciously. Sometimes we aren't even aware that we had them until they are dashed.

Every semester I (Kelli) talk with several students and other twentysomethings who had certain expectations and who are facing the frustrating, and even painful, reality of having those expectations remain unmet. Every semester I hear confessions like the following:

"I *should* be getting an A in this class."

"I *should* have a better job by now."

"I *should* have gotten engaged this spring."

"My roommate and I *should* be better friends."

"Marriage *should* be more fun."

"Our baby *should* be easy."

"My church *should* meet this need."

"(Such-and-such) *should* be faster, nicer, more comfortable or beneficial . . ."

"God *should* be doing this: _____." Fill in the blank.

Such unmet expectations in life are disappointing enough in and of themselves. We thought X *should* happen, and it didn't. But when we put those expectations on another person and we add that relational element to the mix, the results can be downright devastating. I thought so-and-so *should* do this or be that, and so-and-so didn't or wasn't. We feel not only dissatisfied, but hurt and betrayed.

Unmet expectations can also lead to a way of thinking and behaving called "splitting." Splitting happens when we see something or someone as *all* good or *all* bad.[1] It happens when we decide that a good plan is now awful because a single part of it went wrong. Splitting happens when we hate our whole job because one aspect of it becomes difficult. It happens when we abandon a friendship, which delighted us for months or even years, because our friend in some way suddenly stepped out of line. Splitting happens when Peter cleans the whole house—but forgets to wash the windows on the dining room's French doors—and I can *only* see the dirty fingerprints on the glass. Splitting happens when Peter plans a romantic date—but I have to get some work done before we can go—and Peter calls the whole thing off. Splitting happens because we believe that the plan *should* have succeeded and our job *should* be rewarding and other people *should* do exactly as we wish.

LIFE AS IT *SHOULD* BE

So let's talk about that *should*.

How *should* life be?

God knows. He designed the world to be perfect actually.

The word the Bible uses is *shalom*, a word for prosperity and harmony. The opening chapters of Genesis describe a beautiful garden and a beautiful couple in a perfect relationship with one another, with their world, and with God.

If the world met up to God's initial expectations, we would spend every day walking hand in hand with our soul mate in the cool of the day, conversing with Him. Friendly animals of boundless species would frolic at our heels, and a rainbow of flowers would decorate the lush foliage. We would savor a delicious meal of the freshest foods, and all would be well.

So what happened? The Bible reads a bit like a lawyer making a case. First of all, people, you were given a flawless and harmonious environment. But, I'm afraid, you ruined it. Adam and Eve chose self-gratification over their unencumbered communion with God, and humankind's experience of the world was forever changed with the introduction of sin.

Our sin is a horror to God. Our sin twists His creation into a hideous mockery of its original purpose. We have violated His law and His expectations, all of creation is affected by the fall, and what we *deserve* is a torturous death and alienation from Him. We *deserve* for Roman soldiers or temple militia to arrest us. We *deserve* to be beaten beyond recognition and whipped until our back is like a plowed field. We *should* be crucified—asphyxiated and torn to pieces because of the abomination of our sin.

> Let's accept that life is not as great as it possibly could be, and it is not as bad as it could possibly be either.

This is what we *should* expect out of life. The death of Jesus. But God has showered His mercy on us. Jesus died in our stead. He takes our sin. And God is gracious enough to let us live. He keeps the Roman soldiers two thousand years away. He allows much of His creation to continue unflooded and free from plagues and famine. He allows many of us to live in peace and to refrain from massive acts of violence. He allows many of His creatures to enjoy a measure of health and to live a long life. He allows many people to find love and community with family and friends. He allows some of us to invest our time in fulfilling work that brings good to the world. He allows both His followers and those who hate the idea of His existence to craft His creation into beautiful buildings, spectacular music, and compelling pieces of art. He offers us an abundant life in Him. And He calls us to participate in His plan of redemption for the world.

So, in spite of what we deserve, we receive life. And every breath is grace.

GREAT EXPECTATIONS

So what sort of expectations *should* we have?

Popular advice on the subject comes in two categories. Some people say we should set our expectations high. We get what we look for out of life, they argue. People rise to the bar we set, they say. So reach for the stars and look for the sun—since it will always come out. Tomorrow. Bet your bottom dollar.

On the other hand, other people suggest that expecting and planning for the worst scenario in every situation is the safest approach to life. They look to Eeyore as their guide, and they greet each new day as he did: "Good morning, Pooh Bear," said Eeyore gloomily, "if it is a good morning, which I doubt."[2]

While we like Annie and we adore Winnie the Pooh, we

Worralls would advocate a third approach.

Rather than *expecting*, let's think about *accepting*. "Shall we receive good from God, and shall we not receive evil?" (Job 2:10).

ACCEPTING THE GOOD AND THE EVIL

Let's accept that life is full of joy *and* suffering, community *and* isolation, comfort *and* pain. Rather than expecting one or the other, let's accept that we will experience both. Isaiah 45 says, "I form light *and* create darkness, I make well-being *and* create calamity, I am the LORD, who does all these things" (v. 7, emphasis added). Let's accept that life is not as great as it possibly could be, and it is not as bad as it could possibly be either. Let's foster a healthy view that sees life as a mix.

We can also accept this: that whether we like it or not, life is going to go God's way. He will be glorified. Certainly, we can acknowledge our disappointment when our expectations of what God *should* have done have gone unmet. But then we should assess—why would God consider this "good"? Why would God change our plans or obstruct our goals? He may be humbling us. He may be getting our attention. He may be growing us, refining us, preparing us for what is to come. He may be saving us from some unforeseen calamity. Regardless, we need to trust and accept and even expect—that in all things He is working it out for our good (Romans 8:28).

"It is my eager expectation and hope that I will not be at all ashamed, but that with full courage now as always Christ will be honored in my body, whether by life or by death" (Philippians 1:20).

ACTIONS TO CONSIDER

Make a list of things that you expect to happen this week. This year. Divide that list into what you deem to be "good" and "bad" and "neutral."

Ask God to give you contentment and acceptance of whatever the future brings.

QUESTIONS FOR REFLECTION AND DISCUSSION

- Can you think of some ways in which your expectations have been dashed?
- Have you ever engaged in "splitting"?
- What expectations do you have right now—of life? Of other people? Of God?
- Are these expectations realistic and helpful? If not, why not?
- How would your life change if you accepted from God both the good and the bad?

OTHER THINGS TO READ OR WATCH

Acts 20

Jane Austen, *Pride and Prejudice* (Millennium Publications).

Charles Dickens, *Great Expectations* (Penguin Classics) or watch the movie.

C. S. Lewis, *A Grief Observed* (HarperCollins).

#11

TAKE
RISKS

Follow God's leading boldly into the unknown. Heed His call, leaving the outcomes in His hands. As a wise friend advised me when we were contemplating putting our hearts on the line to foster our now-adopted son Daryl, "Do what you won't regret."

> *A ship is always safe at the shore—*
> *but that is not what it is built for.*
>
> —ALBERT EINSTEIN

When I (Peter) was in my teens, my church showed a video sermon by Tony Campolo in which he responds to a study done on fifty people over the age of ninety-five. Participants were asked this question: What would you do differently if you had to live life over again?

The findings were fascinating.

Respondents said they would reflect more. They would do

more things that would live on after they died. But most of all, they said, they would take more risks.[1]

It's that last point that stuck with me the most.

In fact, I was emboldened by that sermon to embrace adventure and experience the world. When I was eighteen, I spent a year in Gujranwala, Pakistan, teaching English. When I was twenty, I spent the summer traveling around the United States with my parents. When I was twenty-three, I moved to Japan to teach English language and culture. When I was twenty-six, I moved back to Pakistan, this time to Murree in the foothills of the Himalayas where I taught fifth grade to the children of missionaries and diplomats. And when I was twenty-eight, I moved to Chicago to study the Bible.

I thought Chicago would be a two-year graduate-school stop, before I headed off to Chile—my next destination. Then a certain undergraduate professor caught my attention, and I've been in Chicago ever since. But that's another story for another time. Actually, you read it toward the beginning of this book.

All that to say, my twenties were a time of new cultures, new friendships, and new landscapes. It was a decade of taking some pretty radical risks. I trekked to the base camp of Nangaparbat mountain, crossed the Batura glacier in the middle of the night, danced for a traditional Japanese dance team, and explored the ruins of the president's palace in Kabul. However, I can see now that all of my galloping around the globe was primarily because my family had taught me to value adventure. I was taking risks for my own sake, not necessarily for God's. And I wasn't always conscious of following His lead.

RISKS OF A DIFFERENT KIND

In the middle of his "If I Had to Live It Over Again" message, Tony Campolo directed his listeners to the hall of heroes in Hebrews chapter 11. It's a list of risk takers, for sure. Noah built a ridiculous boat in the middle of a desert. Rahab hid her enemies in her house. Abraham took off on a trip with no idea about where he was headed. Later, he led his precious son Isaac up the mountain to offer him as a sacrifice.

Pretty radical risks, right?

But these are risks of a different sort than mine. They aren't risks taken simply for the sake of the thrill. They are risks taken "by faith." The chapter repeats that phrase twenty-four times, so it's impossible to miss. They are risks taken in response to the clear call of God. And they are risks which result in a deeper dependence on and relationship with Him.

Moses also appears in Hebrews 11. I (Kelli) have a soft spot for him and the story of his call in Exodus 3 and 4. You've probably heard the story too. In fact, you may have known this narrative since you were a kid. It's included in every Sunday school curriculum and Bible storybook.

I recently asked our son Daryl what he could remember about it. He was able to tell me that God spoke to Moses from a burning bush, that God asked Moses to go to Egypt and rescue His people, that Moses didn't want to go, but he went anyway, that Pharaoh kept changing his mind once Moses got there, that God's people had an "ocean problem," and that God parted the water so His people could pass through. I was duly impressed.

(For the record, I didn't bother to ask our daughter Amelia just yet. She is three, and one Sunday not long ago, when I picked her up from Sunday school and saw her coloring picture of a big fish, she told me excitedly that she had learned about "Jesus and the dolphin." So we have a bit of work to do with her yet.)

Anyhow. Back to Moses.

He was tending his father-in-law's flock, and he led the sheep to the far side of the desert. He ended up—providentially—on the mountain of God. There he was, walking along, minding his own business, tending the sheep, when he noticed a strange phenomenon. A bush, full of flames of fire, but not consumed. It was the angel of the Lord.

GOD ASKED MOSES TO TAKE A RISK, TO FOLLOW HIM BOLDLY INTO THE GREAT UNKNOWN.

Moses didn't know that yet, but he was curious. So he went over to have a closer look.

God saw that He had Moses's attention, and He called to him. "Moses! Moses!"

"Here I am," Moses said.

God said, "Do not come near; take your sandals off your feet, for the place on which you are standing is holy ground" (Exodus 3:5). Then God let Moses know who He was: "I am the God of your father, the God of Abraham, the God of Isaac, and the God of Jacob" (3:6).

At this Moses hid his face, because he was afraid to look at God.

But then the Lord revealed to Moses His motivation for this meeting, and He asked Moses to take a risk, to follow Him boldly into the great unknown.

"I have surely seen the affliction of my people who are in Egypt and have heard their cry because of their taskmasters. I know their sufferings," God said. "And I have come down to deliver them. . . . Come, I will send you" (3:7, 8, 10).

The book of Exodus doesn't give us a visual description of Moses at that point, but I imagine that his eyes bugged out of his head and his jaw hit the ground. Because for the next twenty-nine verses, we hear his repeated protests. The infamous excuses of Moses. Four times he told God why this was not a good plan. Four times he stuttered, "B-b-b-b-but I . . ."

But I'm not worthy. "Who am I?"

But I'm not credible. "What should I say to them?"

But I'm not believable. "What if they don't listen to me?"

But I'm not eloquent. "I'm slow of speech."

Then he finished with his final pathetic plea. "Please send someone else."

After each excuse, of course, we have God's response. Each time God patiently replied—(that is, until Exodus 4:14 when He understandably got a little peeved). God didn't tell Moses, though, what we are often tempted to tell ourselves and our friends when we face a daunting task. He didn't say, "You can do it, Moses! You got this. Don't underestimate yourself. You're gifted. Go, Moses!"

No. Of course not. Rather, each time God responded by completely reorienting Moses. By turning him right around. One hundred and eighty degrees. Each time Moses said, "B-b-b-b-but I . . ." God said, "Behold I . . . !"

"Behold I will be with you."

"Behold I AM WHO I AM."

"Behold I will help you speak."

God promised His presence.

God gave Moses displays of His power. He told Moses to throw his staff on the ground, and it became a snake. He asked him to put his hand inside his cloak, and it became leprous, like snow. Then, too, God declared His purpose. "That they may believe in Me."

A REWARDING RISK

One March afternoon a few years ago, I (Kelli) had a voice-mail message from my friend Tanya, telling us that she had just heard about a seven-month-old baby boy who was "coming up for adoption." She had been praying about it all day, she said, and sensed God leading her to call us.

At the time, our hearts were red raw. We had experienced multiple miscarriages and a few failed adoptions. Our China adoption had been significantly delayed—from two years to six. We had just completed the application and portfolio for a domestic adoption and were moving cautiously in that direction. So this phone call represented another potential change of plans and another potential disappointment.

I told Peter about Tanya's message, and he asked me, "What should we do?"

I replied, "I think we need to call." If we were ever going to be parents, we knew we had to keep taking the risk.

So we called.

Then for the next two weeks we learned all we could about Daryl's situation. He wasn't coming up for adoption; he was coming into the foster system. He might need to be adopted eventually, but he also might return home. No one could say for sure. So of course, the risk for us would be to love him as our own, not knowing if he would actually be ours.

For the next two weeks we sought counsel and prayed and

talked about Daryl. We begged for our own blazing bush. A clear call. I fought back many fears. I voiced all of my excuses. My own, "But . . . but I . . ." I don't know if I can do this. I don't know if I'm ready to risk again. I don't feel strong or brave. I don't want to be disappointed again. I don't want to feel more pain. And I definitely don't *want* to finally love a baby, then have to let him go.

Near the end of the second week of deliberation, I collapsed on a chair in the office of Jan, a colleague and mentor. I told her I was afraid—afraid of making the wrong decision, afraid of suddenly becoming a mom, but also afraid of letting the possibility of this son slip through my fingers because of my fear.

"What should we do?" I asked Jan.

"I don't know, Kelli," she said, sighing. "I guess I would just say, Do what you won't regret."

She didn't give me a chapter and verse, but as we talked, God used her words to remind me of His presence and His promise. "Behold I . . ." I was reminded that God could close the door at any point. He had many times before, and that was His prerogative. But it wasn't our place to preempt Him. God used her words to tell me that—regardless of the result—I would never regret putting myself on the line for baby Daryl. But

We wouldn't trade the front row seat we've had to experience His presence and His power.

I *would* regret it if I didn't. God used those words to show me that if I wanted to see a miracle, I was going to have to throw myself at His mercy. And He used those words to call me—not just into motherhood—but also into something more: a journey of complete surrender and utter dependence on Him. He used those words to tell me what He wanted to give us—not just a child to love—but even more than that, He wanted to give us more of Himself.

So that evening—two weeks after we got the initial information—we called Daryl's caseworker and told her, "We're ready to take the risk. Whatever happens. We want to bring Daryl home."

I wish we could share more here. I wish we could describe for you all of the reasons that risk has paid off, all of the miracles in Daryl's story. I wish I could tell you about all of the moments when God reached in with power and grace and dropped our jaws—providing just the right caseworker at just the right time, giving us favor with a judge and a lawyer and Daryl's birth mom and DCFS. I wish I could explain exactly how God parted the sea of the foster system when no one thought it was possible.

We don't need to say that we wouldn't trade Daryl for the world. He's our son, and we have loved him fiercely since we first laid eyes on his dark curly hair and his darling little dimple and his puddles of drool.

But perhaps we do need to say this: that we wouldn't trade the journey. We wouldn't trade the front row seat we've had to experience His presence and His power. And it has strengthened our belief.

THE FINNYGOOK INN

In Crafthole, a small Cornish village in the United Kingdom, is a fifteenth-century pub called The Finnygook Inn. Near the ceiling, on one of its crossbeams, the following quotation is inscribed:

There is a tide in the affairs of men, which taken at the flood, leads on to fortune.

Omitted, all the voyage of their life is bound in shallows and in miseries.

When I (Peter) first saw this saying, it struck me as true. At that time, I didn't know it was the wisdom of Shakespeare. But the idea of life having an ebb and a flow resonated with me, perhaps in a deeper way because I was raised by the sea.

See, sailors must be prepared for the voyage. Their boats must be watertight. Their sails must be strong. Their provisions must be packed. But there is more to sailing than this. They also have to watch the tide. They can only launch their boat when the tide is in.

He calls each of us to meet Him on holy ground and to be His helpers in rescuing a hurting world.

So it is for us. We have to seize opportunity when it comes. We need to take the risk and leave the land behind, or else we will be stuck in port.

We don't know what specific mission God has called you to or what specific risks He wants you to take in His name. But we do know this. He calls each of us to meet Him on holy ground and to be His helpers in rescuing a hurting world. God speaks from the burning bush and bids us to come on an adventure. As you read this book, right now, the tide is in. Will you cling to the familiar shore? Or will you push off and set your sails to the wind of the Spirit?

You must decide whether or not to take the risk, but as you deliberate, the tide may already be receding across the sand.

ACTIONS TO CONSIDER

Play a game like Monopoly or Risk—and take more chances than you usually would. Tell someone how it felt and what you learned. Sign up for a martial arts class, go on a cross-country road trip, volunteer to lead at your church or serve at a local ministry. Do something that you have thus far been hesitant to do.

Press into a relationship in a bold way. Invite someone new to coffee. Disclose to a trusted friend something you've been wanting to share. Share what God has been teaching you with someone who needs to hear. Resolve a conflict that has lingered for too long and forgive.

QUESTIONS FOR REFLECTION AND DISCUSSION

- What risks have you taken in life? What were the results?
- What excuses have you used for not taking new risks?
- What is the role of the will in taking risks? What is the role of our emotion?
- How have you experienced God's presence when you have followed His call to new places? How has God demonstrated His power in those times? How has your experience of God during times of risk furthered your belief?
- Is God calling you to take a risk right now? If so, is anything holding you back? What would it look like to trust God and push away from shore?

OTHER THINGS TO READ

Exodus 3 and 4
Isaiah 6
Hebrews 11

Tony Campolo, *You Can Make a Difference: High-Voltage Living in a Burned-Out World* (W Publishing Group).

Kevin DeYoung, *Just Do Something: A Liberating Approach to Finding God's Will* (Moody).

Gary Witherall, *Total Abandon* (Tyndale).

#12

EVALUATE YOUR EMOTIONS

They are tricky, and they can be trouble. Often, they spring up from our triggered trauma. For example, let's say (hypothetically) your husband says something about your blog. He might mean it innocently, even positively. But (hypothetically) you hear it differently. You immediately feel threatened, defensive, hurt. All of your (hypothetical) insecurity swells to the surface in an instant. You can go with it. Milk it. Act on it. Hurt him back. Or you can do the better thing and take it back to truth.

Feelings are much like waves; we can't stop them from coming, but we can choose which ones to surf.

—Jonatan Mårtensson

We all have days like this . . .

Roller coaster days. When our emotions whip around—up and down—and threaten to take us along for the ride.

One such memorable day for me (Kelli) was last Good Friday.

Our kids were home from school, and Peter and I were home from work. When they woke up, Daryl and Amelia climbed into the big bed to snuggle for a bit. I squeezed in a short run on the treadmill. After breakfast, we Skyped Peter's mum in England. Then around 10:00 a.m. Peter kicked me out of the house—in the best possible way. He told me to walk down to the Hidden Pearl coffee shop for a while to write. I protested for a moment. Amelia had just sneaked a yogurt and smeared it all over the sofa. But Peter offered to clean it up and insisted that I go. I knew I needed to capitalize on every writing opportunity I could get, so I went.

And it was good. Very good, in fact.

The Hidden Pearl was crowded, but eventually the shop cleared and I was able to claim my favorite table by the window. I soaked in the spring sun, sipped my café au lait, and wrote. I had accepted an invitation to write a Good Friday guest blog about Mary and Martha and Lazarus and Jesus, focusing on Jesus' great love for them and His power over death. And I was so taken with the passage that morning that I praised Him with every tip-tap of the keys.

Finally, late in the afternoon, I packed up my computer and strolled home. Or maybe you could say, I skipped. Or soared even. So amazed was I by Jesus' power and love.

I approached our house, full of anticipation to see my precious family, to share my Good Friday meditations with Peter, and to load the kids in the car and go to church and worship some more.

But as I opened our back gate, something horrible happened.

I took one look at the backyard—at the toys strewn hither and yon, at the cars and trucks and balls and golf clubs and pails and tubs and all manner of water toys. Everywhere. And my heart began to pound. My every muscle tightened. I found it hard to breathe. And I marched up the steps.

The scene in the kitchen wasn't much better. Dirty breakfast and lunch dishes were still in the sink. Crumbs covered the counter. Sand and shoes were piled just inside the back door.

In an instant, a wave of stress and anxiety and anger swelled and crashed around me. I didn't even call out, "I'm home!" I just dropped my bag on the floor and set about the huffy task of putting everything right.

They heard me come in though. My little ones. They came running into the kitchen, calling, "Momma! Momma! You're home!" Of course, their sweet voices tugged at my frustrated frown. But then I saw them. Dirty faces. Dirty hands. Dirty play clothes. And mere minutes before we were to leave for church.

"You're a mess," I groaned, more for Peter's benefit than theirs. He had come to greet me, right on their heels, so I carried on. "I need to get you cleaned up. You can't go to church like that. Hurry up! We have to leave in just a minute." I marched them right up the stairs.

But not before I had made a magnificent mess of my own. Everywhere.

My negative emotions sprayed liberally all over the place. All over the yard. All over the kitchen. All over my family. Up and down the stairs. My furrowed brow. My frowning face. My cutting words. My irritation. My ingratitude. My self-centeredness. My sin.

LAND MINES

When I (Peter) was in Afghanistan for a month, foreign workers were busy finding and destroying hundreds of thousands of mines. During a ten-year occupation, the Soviets had blanketed the country with land mines—buried them in the ground and scattered them all across the land. At that time, UNICEF estimated that there were about forty land mines per square mile, ten million across the entire country. I regularly met people who had lost a leg to a mine. Too many children were killed because they picked up a land mine, thinking it was a toy.

Sometimes dealing with our emotions—and the emotions of those close to us—feels like walking through a minefield. We can be having a happy day or a pleasant conversation. Then a wire gets tripped. A bomb goes off, and suddenly we are sitting in carnage.

Some of us tend to explode, just like those mines. We handle our emotions—anger, frustration, impatience, fear, and even excitement or joy—by displaying them for all to see. If we feel it, we go with it. We embrace it. Feed it. Live it out loud. And everyone around us can't help but notice. The problem with this modus operandi is this: Even if we feel better once we vent, there is no telling what wounds we leave in our wake.

Emotions are a THING THAT WE *have*. THEY are NOT WHO WE *are*.

Others of us, though, actually choose the opposite approach. We withhold our feelings. We deny that we have them—even though we all do. We cut off our emotions. Stuff them. Ignore them. Pretend they don't exist. After a particularly painful experience in my twenties, I (Peter) decided to try this tactic for a time. My emotions had gotten me into trouble, so I decided to do away with them. Yes, I caused less perceptible pain to the people who came across my path. However, I caused deep and lasting damage to myself—physical, emotional, and relational damage—which has taken a long time to undo.

THE REALITY OF EMOTIONS

So how *should* we handle our emotions? What place *should* they have in our lives?

We ought to start by acknowledging them, and owning them, and realizing that we do have a choice regarding how to proceed, realizing that emotions are a thing that we *have*. They are not who we *are*. We possess emotions. Emotions do not possess us. And because we *have* emotions, we can healthily work through them and offer them back to God, who created them in the first place.

We can also eliminate "made" from our emotional vocabulary. "Peter *made* me angry when he didn't clean up the kitchen" is a very different response from this: "When Peter didn't clean up the kitchen, *I* felt angry." The first is an accusation, and we take the role of the passive victim with no power to address the problem. With the latter approach, we acknowledge and own the feeling and are positioned well to process it in a healthy way.

While he doesn't use the specific word "own," Paul implies the importance of emotional ownership in Ephesians 4:26–27 when he says, "Be angry and do not sin; do not let the sun go down on your anger, and give no opportunity to the devil." According to Paul, we have a choice. Yes, we will feel anger. All human beings do, and we ought not to deny it. But—left to fester—anger and other negative emotions can grow like a cancer. So Paul continues by saying, we do *not* have to sin. We do not have to give the devil that foothold. We have that choice.

HANDLING EMOTIONS

A next step to handling emotions is to ask: What exactly *is* the feeling? And what triggered it? It may seem obvious what we feel. Anger. Impatience. Jealousy. Grief. But often the emotion that boils up on the surface is only a reflection of what burns underneath. For example, when I (Kelli) feel a disproportionate amount of anger and frustration that my house and my family are filthy and—consequently—we are going to be late for the Good Friday service at church, the real emotions that I am feeling are fear and a lack of control. I might be—consciously or subconsciously—concerned what the people at church think of my children if they go to church like this. What will the people at church think of *me*? Because on some level I still believe the lie that my worth is affected by my ability to perform. And a perfect performance must include being clean and pressed and punctual.

This is triggering—when an event in the present taps into a past reservoir of pain or anger or fear or shame that has not been healed. It happens when we respond to a current situation with a huge rush of feeling that seems to come from nowhere. A good question we can ask after we have settled down is this: What did that event *mean* to me? We will probably find that the presenting issue is not the *real* issue. For example, if I see dirty dishes in the sink, I may feel a sudden surge of anger. A disproportionate amount—considering there are simply some plates and bowls and spoons and forks covered in a bit of food. They aren't really hurting anything. But the presenting issue is not the *real* issue. The dishes are *not* the problem, but what do they mean to me? What do they represent? What do they trigger? To me, those dirty dishes might be a symbol of disrespect. They might tap into a past reservoir of feeling overlooked or disregarded or taken for granted. They might be a symbol of chaos or confusion or a lack of control. And *that* is what needs to be addressed. My need for control. *That* is what needs to be healed.

Our third step is to evaluate our emotions against truth. We must ask: What do I know to be true about myself? About the other people involved? About this situation? Most important, what do I know to be true about God? When I see those dirty dishes piled high in the sink, I can remind myself that they are just dishes. I can remind myself that Peter loves me. He demonstrates his love and his appreciation for me regularly, in a multitude of ways. This I know to be true. I can remind myself that I am valued—by Peter, yes—but even if that weren't the case, I am valued far more by God. I can also remind myself that a part of loving other people is serving them—whether they show us gratitude or not. I can (calmly) explain my expectations and my concerns. Then, too, I can roll up my sleeves, squirt some detergent, turn on the hot water, and start to scrub.

> Some of our emotions are to be experienced. They are to be felt at their fullest and shared. Grief. Atitude. Joy.

Finally, then, we can give our emotions to God. Some of our emotions are, quite frankly, sin. We can confess those feelings that are not in line with God's will for us. We can nail those feelings to the cross, and He will be faithful to forgive. Some of our emotions are the result of long-standing, deep-rooted pain. We can lay those feelings in His hands, and He will—sometimes slowly, sometimes suddenly—heal. Some of our emotions are to be experienced. They are to be felt at their fullest and shared. Grief. Gratitude. Joy. But even those emotions, we can lay at God's feet. Then He will comfort our broken hearts, receive our worship and our thanks, and ultimately fill our souls with song.

NAIL THOSE FEELINGS TO THE CROSS

Miraculously, we made it to church last Good Friday—almost on time. The kids were relatively clean. And I (Kelli) had tried to apologize to Peter in the car on the short ride over. He forgave me enough that he held my hand as we settled into our seats near the back of the auditorium.

Our church has a Good Friday tradition. Every year they lay a large wooden cross on the stage. The ushers distribute slips of paper and pens, and the pastor invites the congregation to write down their sins and nail them to the rugged beams.

I took my paper. I took my pen. I pulled my coat tight around me. And as the worship team played and other penitents pounded those hammers, I sank low in my seat and cried. Eventually, I scrawled something about my feelings, about letting them get the better of me that day, about my stress and fear and pride and shame—that had been building for weeks and kept bubbling over at the slightest provocation.

Then I rose and went to the front. I stood in the long line, waited my turn, and pierced those things through. I nailed them hard to the cross.

Peter returned to his seat shortly after I did, and in a whispered confession, he told me that his nail had shot away from him on the first stroke, and it had landed on the floor out of reach. As a result, his sins were lying loose on the cross, and he had just re-pounded someone else's sins instead. As a result, when the ushers hoisted the cross to a standing position at the end of the service, Peter's sins fluttered to the floor. Thankfully, my sins stuck.

The next evening our young, newly engaged friends Emma and Ian came to our house for dinner. We talked for hours that night about communication and conflict and expectations and emotions and, in particular, fear. At one point, the darling bride-to-be bemoaned the fact that she had to keep coming back to the same sins, that she hadn't conquered them once and for all. She confessed her frustration that her emotions kept getting the better of her.

I felt her pain. I wanted her to know that she wasn't alone. Though she is forgiven and Spirit-filled, she is still blessedly human. This is life in a fallen world, and this is the painful, but precious, process of spiritual growth.

I told her all about my Not-So-Good Friday. I told her that—even though I have twenty years on her—I still keep circling back to the same old places. The same old hurts. The same old triggers and emotions. The same old sins.

Sometimes those pesky sins flutter back to the floor. But with the help of the Spirit, we pick them up and nail them on again.

But by the grace of God, there is growth. There is growth in the fact that I can usually now see that this is not, in fact, about toys in the yard and crumbs on the counter. It is not even about Peter and how we do or do not share the load. At its core, it is about my fear and control. Good Friday's deep fears over certain things that I could not control made it of utmost importance that I maintain extra tight control over the things that I could.

But it goes even deeper than that. Stretches further back. This is an old pattern. These are old tapes, playing in my head and triggering my old fears of worth and identity. My old desires for perfection and approval and my old emotions of anger and frustration kick in without any thought.

By the grace of God, however, there is growth. There is growth when I seek to acknowledge my feelings—to own them and release them and seek forgiveness and nail them on the cross. There is growth when I make peace with the fact that sanctification doesn't always mean we get to cross our sins off the list for good. No. Unfortunately, not. Sometimes those pesky sins flutter back to the floor. But with the help of the Spirit, we pick them up and nail them on again.

ACTIONS TO CONSIDER

Talk to a friend or family member about your emotional life in general and about how you are feeling right now specifically. What good can come of simply expressing these things to another person?

Journal your emotions. Then evaluate—is this emotion appropriate for the situation? Is it proportionate? Is it helpful? Is it healthy? Does God have anything to say about it? Does it honor Him? Or might it even be sin?

QUESTIONS FOR REFLECTION AND DISCUSSION

- Do you tend to display your emotions or deny them?
- Can you think of a time recently when it would have been helpful for you to "own" your emotions? How might the situation have gone differently?
- Can you think of a time recently when you were "triggered"? When you responded to a present situation with a disproportionate amount of emotion? Describe what happened. What reservoir of past pain was being triggered?
- What do you know to be true in this situation? About yourself? About the other people involved? About God? Bring that past pain to God. Ask Him to heal those places.

OTHER THINGS TO READ

Philippians 4

Bill Gillham, *Lifetime Guarantee: Making Your Christian Life Work and What to Do When It Doesn't* (Harvest House).

Dallas Willard, *Renovation of the Heart: Putting on the Character of Christ* (NavPress).

13

PRESS INTO PAIN

While no one wants to experience pain, you will. Don't be shocked. Don't run from it. Don't ignore it. Don't fight it. Let it burn. Let it melt your heart. But never fear that God has abandoned you to the flame. He is there. His presence is unwavering. He is pursuing you and purging the dross. You are not being punished. You are being purified.

> *I tear down to rebuild. And through the process of pain, growth happens. I hate it, but it is good.*
>
> —HENRY CLOUD, *HOW PEOPLE GROW*

I (Kelli) just watched a video montage of several buildings being demolished. One minute they were standing there—these enormous structures of brick and concrete and steel. Then suddenly they exploded, then imploded, then crumbled to the ground.

Some of you have experienced firsthand this violent sort of tearing down—not of a physical structure, but of your life. Some of you have survived a singular knee-buckling day when the world, as you knew it, exploded, then imploded, then came crashing down. And you were left, covered in debris, reeling in the rubble and the ruin.

So far our experience of pain hasn't been quite like that. We haven't experienced one momentous tragedy or one utterly devastating day. So far, for Peter and me, pain has come as a more systematic deconstruction. More crowbars and sledgehammers than dynamite. We've had to acknowledge and grieve several sorrows from our past, and we've had our share of heartache in our present. We've lost parents to cancer, some friends to faulty communication and conflict, and three babies we never had the pleasure of holding—to name a few.

PAIN IN MANY PACKAGES

Pain comes in many packages. It sometimes takes us by surprise. It sometimes comes as the logical and long-anticipated consequence of our own choices. It sometimes comes simply as the inevitable outworking of life in a fallen world.

Some pain begins as physical pain. I (Peter) have recently sought treatment for my back and my stomach and my head; I've had chronic pain in all of these places. Both of Kelli's parents spent their whole lives navigating the physical limitations of cerebral palsy. Those of you living with physical pain know that it bleeds into the emotional and the spiritual realm as well.

I recently discovered the story of Pastor Ed Dobson. In 2000, Pastor Dobson was diagnosed with ALS (Amyotrophic Lateral

Sclerosis), a neurodegenerative disease that affects the nerve cells in the brain and the spinal cord. At the time he was enjoying a vibrant pastoral ministry, and he anticipated many more years of service. With ALS, however, the brain progressively loses its ability to control muscle movement, and as the patient's muscles receive decreased input from the brain, they waste away. The standard life expectancy for a person with ALS is two to five years. So because of ALS, Ed lost not only control of his body—but he also lost his identity.

Some pain comes as a result of our relationships. It may begin in our past. It may look like neglect, abuse, or a lack of bonding. Regardless, it will undoubtedly leak into our present. My friend David is just one example of this. David never knew his birth father. During most of David's childhood, his mother and stepfather were active in church. However, when the stepfather lost a close relative, he withdrew from the family, self-medicated with alcohol and TV, and turned his back on his faith. After a few too many drinks, David's stepfather would often tell David that he should be more grateful, saying things such as, "I've provided for you all these years and you're not even my son."

David's mother did her best to carry on and support David, but she struggled too. She and David's stepfather separated multiple times. Their marriage was perpetually rocky. And in the midst of her own pain, she too has struggled with her faith.

So although he has been provided for financially, David has not always been provided for emotionally. He has watched his primary spiritual role models give up on the faith. Now in his twenties, David wants to follow God. However, he feels helpless to handle the pain he feels at being estranged from his own home. David wrestles with guilt and grief. He longs for intimacy,

O BSERVING THIS LEVEL OF PAIN AND DESPAIR CAUSED ME TO ASK, HOW COULD GOD ALLOW SUCH EVIL?

but he also finds it frightening.

Some pain hurts our head. When I (Peter) was in Pakistan at the age of eighteen, I wrestled intensely with my faith. I asked myself why I believed the Bible was true. A friend told me with great conviction that Jesus accepted the Bible as true and so should we. But I immediately recognized that my friend was quoting the Jesus of the Bible to support belief in the Bible. In my mind, the logic didn't hold up. People all around me in Pakistan believed that the Qur'an was true. If I had been raised in Pakistan, I thought, wouldn't I be defending the Qur'an as the word of God?

Then I saw beggars on the street with twisted limbs and open sores. I heard that some of the beggars may have been intentionally hurt by someone they knew in order to evoke more sympathy. The beggar who evokes more sympathy receives more money. Observing this level of pain and despair caused me to ask, How could God allow such evil?

A dull ache formed in my temples and spread across the front of my head. I couldn't make sense of why people would believe the tenets of Christianity. Each morning of that long year I would wake up free from the ache, but then I would have my first conscious thoughts, and they would be thoughts of doubt. I would once again deconstruct my faith in my own mind. It would unravel in my head until the Bible lost its authority. Jesus became a mythical legend, a historical figure we knew little about. God was just a concept that was slipping from view.

Some pain sears our soul. We had only been in our new house for one week when I (Kelli) discovered that I was pregnant for the first time. I was home alone when I took the test and saw the two pink lines appear in the screen. I was shocked and amazed. We had been trying for two years. That meant two years of monthly heartbreak, needles and pills, and trips to the clinic. But for me it also meant two years of railing against the God I blamed for all of it. The God who seemed so silent. The God who now saw fit to give me the desire of my heart in spite of my rage.

Bursting with the news, I went shopping, intent on finding a meaningful way to tell Peter. For the first time in two years, I didn't avoid the baby section. I walked straight there with my head held high and tears burning hot in my eyes. I lingered in those aisles. And for the first time I allowed myself to melt over the itty-bitty socks and fuzzy blankets.

Eventually, I tore myself away from bath toys and bottles and took my quest to the toy section where I found just the right thing. A tiny, blue soccer ball. Peter loves soccer. One of his fatherly dreams has always been to teach his children the game. And now, I was finally able to make that dream come true. I bought the ball and a gift bag and a card that said, "Congratulations."

That evening I met Peter at the door. Beaming. I took his hand and pulled him into the study. I pushed him into one of the wingback chairs and handed him the gift bag.

"What's the occasion?" he asked, eyeing me with suspicion.

"Just open it," I said.

He reached in and pulled out the toddler-sized soccer ball first. "Okay?" he said.

I just smiled, waiting for the penny to drop. "There's a card," I said.

He pulled out the envelope, opened the card, and read my

message: "Congratulations, Coach! This is to help you train up Baby Worrall."

"What?" Peter said, clearly afraid to believe it was true.

"I took two tests," I told him. "Both positive. One is in the bag."

He dug back in the bag and pulled out the stick. He stared at the two pink lines, then he looked up at me, his eyes wide with disbelief. We both stood up and wrapped our arms tightly around each other. We stood there in silence for a long time. He kissed my face.

"Finally," he whispered in my ear. "Finally."

Three weeks later I miscarried.

PERSPECTIVES ON PAIN

When we're in the midst of pain and suffering, we often ask questions: Will I make it through? And how? What will life look like on the other side? How can an all-powerful God allow such suffering? How can He stand so silently by? Who is He in the midst of this? And does this pain serve any good purpose?

GRIEF IS THE MOST IMPORTANT PAIN OF ALL BECAUSE IT LEADS US TO THE PLACE OF COMFORT AND HEALING. IT TAKES US TO THE FOOT OF THE CROSS.

The nihilist would say no. And truthfully, when the destruction is all you can see, it's tempting to agree with him. When I (Kelli) learned of our first miscarriage, as I lay in our bed—curled in a tight little ball—trembling with fear and anger and grief, I certainly didn't see any positive point.

But there is another perspective.

Does pain serve a purpose? C. S. Lewis says, "Yes. It does." In fact, he saw pain as a central component to spiritual formation. In *The Problem of Pain*, he famously wrote, "God whispers to us in our pleasures, speaks in our conscience, but shouts in our pain: it is His megaphone to rouse a deaf world."[1]

Does pain serve a purpose? Henry Cloud and John Townsend say, "Yes. It most certainly can." In their book *How People Grow*, they make a distinction though. Between good pain and bad. Between therapeutic suffering that brings life change, "destructive suffering at the hands of evil people," and worthless suffering that persists unnecessarily, that we perpetuate when we refuse to face our own stuff.[2] The trick is telling the difference.

Cloud and Townsend would say that God uses good pain—and grief—to produce in us growth. In fact, they call grief "the pain that heals all of the rest."[3] Grief is the most important pain of all because it leads us to the place of comfort and healing. It takes us to the foot of the cross. And when we grieve well, the good pain can do its good work. It can push our old coping mechanisms past their breaking point. It can tear down parts of our character, make space for the new, open up places that another season of comfort never could, and prepare us to live as we were designed to live.

Does pain serve a purpose? George Barna also says, "Yes. It does." In his book *Maximum Faith,* he outlines ten stops in the spiritual path. Stop Number 7 on this journey toward maximum faith is "Personal Brokenness." Stop 6 is a "Prolonged Period of Spiritual Discontent." And perhaps it is only a time of brokenness that can break us free from our extended dissatisfaction.

"Brokenness" is something of a buzzword these days. It's used in Christian circles to mean a variety of things. Sometimes it simply describes the human condition. We are all "broken." Sinful. A great big mess. Or it describes our emotional state when the pain is just too much. Or it describes our families, our homes, when relationships dissolve.

Barna's definition is a bit different though. He describes "brokenness" as a specific time of face-to-face confrontation—between God and us. When "God meets [believers] head-on with the realization that they are still too self-reliant."[4] When God allows a period of pain, wanting to evoke in us a response of "reflection and meditation, sorrow and remorse, realistic self-evaluation, talking and listening to [Him], and coming to the end of self."[5] And it is only through this sort of brokenness that we are prepared for the "glorious healing and reconstruction that God has in mind."[6]

Does pain serve a purpose? Robert Sears of Loyola University would also say, "Yes. It does." In fact, he has said that our understanding of suffering is a key indicator of our spiritual maturity.[7] Those who are young in their journey of faith often see suffering as punishment. When they experience pain, they think, "I have done a bad thing. I am being punished." In the mind of a less mature believer, we live in a world of crime and punishment. We get the justice we deserve. However, as we mature, we grow to understand that perfect love casts out all fear and fear has to do with punishment (1 John 4:18). Jesus' disciple John teaches us this. He saw Jesus on the cross, taking the punishment for all those who follow Him. But we do not need to be fearful of God preparing the gallows for us and stringing us up for public display. Our punishment has already been served.

According to Sears, the next stage in our understanding of suffering is to see suffering as discipline. Sometimes pain *is* meant to call us back. Sometimes when we are heading down a dangerous path, the pain that results from our bad choices is designed to steer us back on course. When this is the case, we do well to respond quickly to the goad. We do well to own the error, seek forgiveness, and return to the right road.

When Kelli and I became foster parents, we had to take a ten-week parenting course. One entire session focused on the difference between punishment and discipline. The distinction is this: Punishment often shames and leaves the child isolated. Punishment fits the crime, but it is not redemptive. Discipline, instead, instructs and dialogs. Discipline tries to get to the root of the issue and nip unhealthy behavior at its source. Discipline digs deeper than punishment, and it is redemptive. Punishment can ultimately kill us—body and soul. Discipline brings us to life.

We can also think of discipline in the sense of exercising our muscles, making ourselves strong. We feel physical pain

> To be afraid of discipline is to remain weak and immature. To embrace discipline is to grow through pain into someone who is wise, strong, and well-respected.

when we start a new physical workout, but we discipline ourselves in order to train and improve. The same is true spiritually. The author of Hebrews says that no discipline seems pleasant at the time, but God disciplines us as His children because He loves us. As a caring Father He doesn't stand by and let His children become whatever kind of misfit they want to be. Rather, He corrects them and redirects them. It doesn't feel good. It can even feel a lot like punishment, but it has a purpose and the purpose is worth the pain. To be afraid of discipline is to remain weak and immature. To embrace discipline is to grow through pain into someone who is wise, strong, and well-respected.

Sears's third stage in the understanding of suffering is to use it as a witness. If the greatest call on a person's life is to serve God, then the greatest result of pain is that it will point to God. In #8, Be Patient, we saw this in the story of Mary and Martha and Lazarus in John 11. Jesus told His disciples multiple times that Lazarus's death would result in the glory of God. He also explained that the goal of the glory of God was so that the people might believe.

You can read and watch movies about Ed Dobson's journey with ALS at his website (edsstory.com). There it says, "Suffering is everywhere and it changes us, for better or worse. . . . [Here] Ed wrestles with issues suffering raises: worry, identity, forgiveness, gratitude, and healing. Emerging from it all is his discovery that there is always hope."[8] Ed's approach to the painful reality of a wasting disease has been to embrace gratitude and to share that gratitude and hope with others. Ed's story has reached thousands of people with the truth of God's grace in the midst of pain. Ed's pain is a witness of God's glory, and it has brought many to belief.

A final view of suffering, according to Robert Sears, is vicarious suffering. This is similar to suffering as witness, but it has a more specific target. Vicarious suffering is experienced in place of another person. When we recognize that we may possess privilege and position, we can embrace that privilege or we can give it away.

In *A Tale of Two Cities* Charles Dickens tells the story of good-for-nothing Sydney Carton, who decides to sacrifice himself to the guillotine so that others will be saved. As he stares death in the face, he imagines the lives of those he seeks to save.

And his last unspoken thought is this: "It is a far, far better thing that I do, than I have ever done; it is a far, far better rest that I go to than I have ever known."[9]

The story points toward Robert Sears's final stage of vicarious suffering. Ultimately, we look to Jesus as the perfect example of this sort of suffering. Jesus, who had the highest privilege of being the Son of God enthroned in heaven and who gave it all up for us. So that we didn't have to be damned forever, He emptied Himself and endured death. It wasn't just any kind of death. It was the kind of death reserved for the worst of criminals.

Hundreds of years before Jesus was born on this earth, Isaiah prophesied about His pain. "He was despised and rejected by men; a man of sorrows, and acquainted with grief; and as one from whom men hide their faces he was despised, and we esteemed him not" (Isaiah 53:3). God descended into the world of suffering and is still present in this world of pain. He knows our sorrows. When we scream into the cosmos that we have been abandoned, He is right by our side. Our processing of pain must begin with that truth. Jesus knows.

ACTIONS TO CONSIDER

Engage in a physical activity and push past your usual pain threshold. What can you learn from this?

QUESTIONS FOR REFLECTION AND DISCUSSION

- When have you felt intense pain (physical, emotional, or mental)?
- Did you make sense of the pain? What did you learn?
- What pain might you need to press into right now?
- How might God grow you if you press into that pain?

OTHER THINGS TO READ

Job

John 4

George Barna, *Maximum Faith: Live Like Jesus* (Fedd and Company).

Henry Cloud and John Townsend, *How People Grow: What the Bible Reveals about Personal Growth* (Zondervan).

Charles Dickens, *A Tale of Two Cities* (Barnes and Noble Books).

C. S. Lewis, *The Problem of Pain* (Macmillan).

#14

TAKE SIN SERIOUSLY

There is no such thing as "getting away with it"—even if you don't "get caught." Though grace is gigantic and forgiveness is free, sin does still stain. And the spot will undoubtedly spread further and sink deeper than you can initially see.

> *One great power of sin is that it blinds men so that they do not recognize its true character.*
>
> —ANDREW MURRAY

Don and Viv were married when she was twenty and he was twenty-one. Don worked at a company called Gleason's, operating gear cutters and running machines. Not long before they married, Viv suffered from an extended illness and lost her secretarial job, so money was particularly tight in the early years. Regardless, with the help of a loan from Viv's father, they managed to purchase a small semidetached (duplex) home in Deeble

Close, Plympton, England. And they settled into (a sometimes happy, sometimes not) married life.

I (Peter) was born less than two years later.

My earliest memories are located in that semidetached house in Deeble Close. The foundations of my life were formed there. I have fond memories of playing with my soldiers on the old stone fireplace that my dad had built. My German Mountain Troops would climb up to the mantelpiece where they had their Alpine base. I remember the sun shining through my bedroom curtains, painting glowing shapes on my walls. And I remember lying on my bed and listening to the rumble of the diesel trains as they strained up Hemerdon Bank, taking passengers to London or pulling china clay to the kilns.

But I have other memories as well. Some not so pleasant ones. In a particularly powerful picture, one that is seared most deeply on my brain, I am sitting on the landing, looking down the stairs at a pane of broken glass. I am three, maybe four.

My father is looking dejected. He's pacing the hall, and my mother is gone.

The euphoria of their teenage love had quickly worn off for Don and Viv, my dad and mum. My father still expected the world to revolve around him as it had in his boyhood days, and my mother didn't want to be anyone's slave. He thought marriage was supposed to make his life better, and she wanted to matter more to him than it seemed she did. Power and control. Expectations and disappointment. Intimacy and loneliness. These are the familiar struggles at the center of a young marriage.

Though they weren't aware, I heard their conversations on the other side of my wall. Words from their bedroom crept into mine. Regrets and recriminations. Something about my dad not being the marrying kind. He won arguments by scraping up muck and cathartically casting it at the object of his scorn. When he felt better, he would come back and expect forgiveness and affection. But the muck he slung had stuck. My mother was losing the fight against his rage and her sanity.

> **I DIDN'T FORGET THAT IMAGE OF THE DOOR AND THE WINDOW AND MY DAD AND THE SNOW.**

That night, then, they had both raised their voices, and she had decided to leave. The door slammed. The window next to it shattered. Snow was falling, and some blew in through the hole. I sat at the top of the stairs, looking down at Dad's despondency and feeling forgotten in the fray. But I didn't forget that image of the door and the window and my dad and the snow. Nor did I forget the feeling of fear that accompanied it.

One time, to make amends, my father went to Mum's childhood home and was humble enough to face his mother-in-law, the formidable Myrtle May. She met my father at the door, and he courageously announced that he had come to get his wife. Undoubtedly, my grandmother gave him a tongue-lashing.

And so it went. Over and over, my father won my mother back with his persistence but lost her in the moments. Over and over, though they loved each other in their own wild way, they also hurt each other in ways that scarred. And over and over—as it is with all parents—but unbeknownst to them, their sin also left its mark on me.

SIN: THE NEXT GENERATION

My twenties looked different from my dad's in several significant ways.

I wasn't "tied down" by a mortgage or a wife or a child. I didn't work at one steady manufacturing job for years on end. Instead, I lived the life of a bachelor, a world traveler, an adventurer of sorts. I taught school and worked with NGOs and played soccer and climbed mountains and hit the clubs with my friends at night. I was free and unattached and able to do as I pleased. And as I moved from England to Japan to Pakistan during that decade, as I traveled all around Europe and Asia and even as far as Australia, I too often made decisions based on what would satisfy me. In that way, I suppose, I was a chip off the old block.

I struggled with insecurity back then. (Still do.) But rather than work through my insecurity with a Christian counselor or prayerfully find ways to see my worth in Christ, I focused on getting my next girlfriend to meet that need.

I loved the rush of excitement when a girl agreed to go on a date, and I felt momentarily safe and content when she became my girlfriend officially. However, to keep the high going, I had to make compromises, and I became fixated. The girl quickly consumed my thoughts. I spent every possible moment in her presence. I wrote her long poems, praising her looks and her personality. And even though I would try to choose someone who called herself a Christian, our focus wasn't on walking with God. Our focus was on romance, and the relationships became increasingly physical and increasingly obsessive as time went by.

Then there would be the inevitable moment of discord. That sudden dissatisfaction. A period of disillusionment. When the blinders would fall and I would see the relationship as it really was. I would sense our incompatibility. I would see my own addiction. I would realize that I had lost my focus on God, and I would become afraid.

Most often this resulted in a painful breakup at about the four-month mark.

Ridiculously, though, when the loneliness and the self-loathing threatened to overwhelm, I would go back, cap in hand, to the same girl. If she accepted me, the cycle would simply repeat. If she did not, I would feel despair and rejection on an even deeper level than before.

Many of us imagine that walking down that aisle will bring us all of the security we long for.

And so it went. Over and over, my relationships delivered an immediate reward but never the ultimate life I was searching for. Over and over, I ended up more insecure rather than less, more focused on meeting my own needs than loving someone else. Over and over, I hurt these girls and they hurt me in ways that scarred. And unbeknownst to me, I would carry the residual effects of my sin into my marriage as well.

Before we marry, many of us imagine that walking down that aisle will bring us all of the security we long for. However, I was even more insecure during periods of my marriage than I had been in my twenties. I was afraid and defensive at times, so I didn't lead well. I didn't contribute well. And when things became particularly difficult, I sometimes embraced a pattern of escape. I would idealize the relationships that I once had, and I would go back to them in my mind and even in my dreams. In my imagination, I would cling to the self-worth and acceptance I thought I once had. And rather than building into my marriage, I built a godless sanctuary in my subconscious that cast its shadow on our home.

And so it went. Over and over, the sometimes subtle and sometimes obvious cycle of sin.

A SAD TALE OF SIN

For over a year, I have been preaching on and off at a small church in Woodstock, Illinois, the next town over from ours. Several months ago we started in Genesis and are working our way through the Bible. Beginning to end. This morning I preached from 1 Samuel 13.

The early reign of King Saul. A sad tale of sin.

Saul has come to the throne for one reason alone: to lead Israel in battle against her enemies. He has already triumphed over the Ammonites in chapter 11. And the passage makes it clear that this victory was accomplished in the power of the Spirit of God (v. 6). The prophet Samuel even says, "Today *the* LORD has worked salvation in Israel" (v. 13 emphasis added).

In today's sermon from chapter 13, the Israelites are facing another formidable foe: the Philistines, who instigated this conflict when they stole the ark of the covenant in 1 Samuel chapters 4–7.

So here's the scene in chapter 13. Saul has an army of three thousand men. Two thousand are with him at Micmash, and the other thousand are with his son Jonathan across the way. In verse 3, Jonathan's division launches an attack. Saul orders a trumpet to be blown so that all of Israel knows that they are at war.

When the people hear that signal, they are understandably concerned. And when they see that the Philistines have assembled "thirty thousand chariots and six thousand horsemen and troops like the sand on the seashore in multitude" (13:5), it is no surprise that many of them run and hide.

Saul is left in Gilgal with a handful of troops, quaking in fear. He waits like this for seven long days, the amount of time the prophet Samuel had instructed. But Samuel doesn't come, and Saul's pitiful army starts to scatter. Then Saul takes matters into his own hands.

"Bring me the burnt offering," he says.

Then, just as he finishes making the sacrifice, Samuel shows up. He asks, "What have you done?"

Of course, Saul defends his decision. He justifies his fear. He blames Samuel's delay. He even tries to bring God into it. "I hadn't sought the Lord's favor," he explains.

But Samuel doesn't buy it one bit. "You acted foolishly," Samuel says. "You didn't keep the command of the Lord." Plain and simple. And there will be consequences. Saul's kingdom would collapse.

THE CYCLE

I happen to be reading through 1 Samuel right now, and I notice something about chapter 13. It's the same cycle we see throughout Scripture. Over and over, from Genesis through Revelation, the biblical characters are tempted. And they sin. And they suffer the devastating effects. And they repent. And they are restored. Until they are tempted again. Over and over, it's the same cycle we experience as well. As did our parents. As will our children. And so it goes.

But most of us don't set out to "sin," and most of us don't count the cost.

No, sin is more subtle than that.

It begins with a desire. A natural desire, and a human one. For pleasure. For power. Or perhaps control. For order. Or significance. Or freedom from what binds. We want relief from pain. We long for acceptance and safety and happiness, for security and love. And of course, many of these desires are even good.

But then, as Saul did—and as I did too—we get impatient for that desire to be fulfilled. We feel pressured—by a threatening army and an impending attack. By a ticking clock or by our persistent peers or by the desire itself. And our knees wobble. Desperation sets in. We doubt ourselves and our ability to live well without that thing. We doubt our God, too, and His willingness to help. We doubt His strength, His timing, and His love. We lose hope and any capacity to hold on to truth.

And then we take matters into our own hands—sometimes consciously, sometimes subconsciously. Sometimes we drift as much as decide. Regardless, we fulfill that desire in our own way or in our own time. But at what cost? There will be consequences. Our kingdom will collapse.

So it goes.

But there is grace. (Keep reading.)

ACTIONS TO CONSIDER

Take one day and choose not to defend yourself against people who question your behavior or character. Instead of contradicting them, restate what you think they are saying. What do you learn about your own sin nature?

Pray Psalm 32 or Psalm 51.

Verbally acknowledge your sin before God. Make amends with other people where appropriate.

Questions for Reflection and Discussion

- How have you observed or experienced the consequences of sin?
- How have you seen the consequences of sin spill over from one generation to another?
- Which of the desires listed above do you resonate with right now?
- How might you be tempted to fulfill those desires in the wrong ways or in the wrong time?
- How could you treat sin more seriously in ways that are distinctly Christian?

Other Things to Read

Genesis 3 and 4

1 Samuel 13

Graham Greene, *The End of the Affair* (Penguin Books).

Flannery O'Connor, *A Good Man Is Hard to Find and Other Stories* (Harcourt).

Mary Shelley, *Frankenstein* (Barnes and Noble Classics).

15

EMBRACE GRACE

Accept it with open arms and open heart. Hold it tight until it soaks into your soul. Then release it. Give it away. To your family, to your friends, to your church. When I (Kelli) was a twentysomething, my church was falling apart. The pastor left. The leadership couldn't agree. The congregation was about to split. I was disillusioned and critical, sitting in judgment over all of them, looking down my nose with disgust. But that posture helps no one, and it is not your place. Instead, be a conduit for grace.

> *Amazing grace! How sweet the sound,*
> *that saved a wretch like me.*
>
> —JOHN NEWTON

I (Peter) sat in an auditorium. Weeping. My shoulders heaved as I sensed God's grace wash over me. I wasn't in a revival meeting or a worship service. I was in the front row of a performance of *Les Miserables*.

In Victor Hugo's famous story of redemption, the protagonist Jean Valjean is arrested for stealing a crust of bread to feed his sister's seven children. Yes, his arrest is just, but it seems severe since the family was starving.

Jean Valjean's original sentence is for five years. But because he tries to escape four different times, the sentence repeatedly gets extended, and he ultimately spends nineteen years in the harsh prison environment. When he is finally released, he is a changed man. Hardened and cold.

When Valjean arrives in the town of Dinge, the "yellow passport" he must carry as an ex-convict makes it difficult for him to secure lodging. Everyone turns him away, until the kind Bishop Myriel finally takes him in. The bishop feeds him supper and gives him a bed, but then—in the middle of the night—Valjean steals the bishop's silverware and silver plates and tries to sneak out of town. He is caught, however, and hauled back to the bishop by the police. Certainly, the bishop could rightfully accuse Valjean of theft and send him back to prison. But he doesn't.

I can still picture the Bishop Myriel in that production—standing in his nightclothes. The dramatic stage lights illuminated his face as he told the police that he had given Valjean the silverware and the silver plates. And, the bishop said, it was fortunate that Jean Valjean had returned because he had left the silver candlesticks behind, and they were the most valuable items of all. The bishop then tells Valjean that—with the candlesticks—he has purchased Valjean's life and he should live accordingly. Of course, Valjean's hard heart softens. And he is, once again, changed. This time by grace. He spends his life working on behalf of the impoverished and caring for an orphan girl.[1]

And in the front row of that theater, I wept. Because I am just like Jean Valjean. I, too, have been tangled in sin. But I, too, have been bought by grace. I, too, have been uplifted by Jesus to live a life that is so much better than I deserve.

So have you.

PERSISTENT GRACE

Grace abounds. It is in every new morning, every generous act, every breath we breathe.

God's common grace keeps the world spinning on its axis and causes the sun to shine without preference. Every man, woman, and child knows something of this sort of grace.

But the fullness of God's grace comes through Jesus. His death and resurrection bring redemption to those who receive Him and confess His name. When we were slave to our sin, He bought us back. When we were imprisoned, He set us free. When we spat in His face, He extended His hand. Neither the muck and mire of our depravity nor the magnitude of His grace can be overstated.

But grace isn't for the flippant or the casual. It isn't to be trampled or treated lightly or taken for granted. Yet, we all do this.

I know I did. For many years I didn't understand what was so amazing about grace. I didn't understand what was so destructive about my sin. I didn't understand that I needed that grace—not just at the point of my salvation. No. I needed it to live every day. I didn't understand any of that—until I felt condemned again—years *after* I had been saved.

I sat in the lofty, cold, gospel hall of my home church in England. I had asked to meet with the elders because I needed to confess my sin. My heart pounded in my chest, and I could hear my pulse in my ears.

I had previously lived powerfully for Jesus. I had been the church's golden boy, the one who invited his friends along and saw them come to the faith.

But my image was about to be tarnished—no, shattered.

After I shared with the elders how I had fallen from grace, after I confessed the choices that I had made and explained the already evident consequences, they began to deliberate. One elder said that love covers a multitude of sin and that I should be supported, forgiven, and restored in quick fashion. A couple of the elders seemed confused and stayed silent. But one elder took a sterner approach. He pressured the others to have my sin announced from the pulpit. He wanted to expel me from the congregation for a time as an example to those who had looked up to me.

They didn't expel me. And my bond to the church ran so deep that I couldn't bring myself to leave. So I continued to attend the Sunday morning meetings, during which members of the congregation gave out hymns, Bible readings, or personal testimonies as they felt led. Although the elders said plenty to God in the months that followed my confession, they said very little to me. Every Sunday the congregation sat in regimented rows, like tombstones, and I took my place in the back row—sadly staring at my shoes and waiting for the hour to pass.

We were a ragtag bunch, who were far from righteous, but we had a hunger for God.

During this time, though, I did continue to gather young

people around me, those who struggled with the same issues I did, and we started praying for the church. We gathered every Saturday night in the "upper room" of the church, and we sat in a circle and prayed. We were a ragtag bunch, who were far from righteous, but we had a hunger for God.

I remember praying that the church would stop using the old black hymnal. Its pages were yellowed and *The Believer's Hymnal* was embossed in gold letters on its cover. Those words looked to me like the gold nameplate on a black coffin. It symbolized age and irrelevance, and every song sounded like a funeral dirge. I wanted to sing from the *new* songbook that had been introduced in recent years. It seemed to have some life. However, God changed our own hearts through our time of prayer, and I began to see what the old saints saw in their old book. I even gave out a hymn or two for the church to sing.

Gradually, we young people started participating more in the service. Gradually, I realized that, even as a broken sinner, I had something to contribute. God had changed me and used me to encourage change in others. Gradually, I understood more of what it means to live by grace rather than by my own strength.

One Sunday night, shortly before I graduated from college, the young people were crammed into a small house for their after-church meeting. I had a lot of questions about faith in those days. And the trite, easy answers rarely satisfied my hunger for truth. That night was no different, and the meeting had barely begun when I disagreed with something that was said.

One of the elder's daughters—the elder who had wanted me expelled from the church—was distraught that I was once again questioning matters of the faith, and she left the meeting upset. Wanting to make amends, I went to her house to apologize. I rang the doorbell and waited for a reply. What followed left me scarred for years and painfully afraid of church people.

The elder and his wife pulled me into their house. They sat me down, and for more than two hours they recounted all of my faults. They let me know that since I was ten, they had thought I was odd. I read Christian books that no one else read. I seemed happy when other people were sad. They were not surprised that I kept disagreeing with people at the youth meetings since I had never seemed to fit the mold. They told me I needed to keep quiet in the church. They told me I should never work with youth. And they made me promise not to tell anyone about our conversation as others might not agree.

Then the elder drove me home. Calmly he apologized for the emotional nature of the outburst at his home. He attributed that to the women in the house. He did, however, reiterate that—at the age of twenty-two—my days of ministry in any church were over.

I was preparing to move to Japan, but for my last few weeks in England, the other elders in the church noticed the abrupt change in my demeanor and my sudden lack of participation in the church. They asked if that elder had spoken to me. They wanted to speak with him if he had. But since he had sworn me to secrecy, I said nothing.

In spite of the inappropriate way all of this happened, I see these events as the foundation for my understanding of grace.

The elder and his family did not show me grace. Rather, they convinced me that I had nothing to give. In the many years

> Because I knew both condemnation and grace, I felt prepared to preach grace to them.

since that time, I have become aware that I do have boundless resources to pass on, but not because of anything special in me. It is because God uses the humble. When I was brought low, God began to raise me up and use me as a teacher.

I decided, eventually, that I needed more Bible training, and I attended seminary. While I was there, God—in His grace—took the healing deeper. I raised my hand in class, and with some fear and trembling I asked the same questions that had previously brought me condemnation. My professors responded with grace. They gently gave me answers, and God used them to tend to my soul. As I was discipled, rather than punished, I was changed.

When I graduated from seminary, God called me to pastor a small church. Some people in our congregation struggled with sin which, in the eyes of some, may have made my sin seem like child's play. However, because I knew both condemnation and grace, I felt prepared to preach grace to them.

My relationship with my home church in England has been redeemed by grace as well. After nine years, the church wrote me a formal letter, stating that I was in good standing with them. They have even asked me to preach there when I have been back to visit.

So in spite of all that I deserve, and in spite of all that has brought me pain, God has worked in His grace to give me more than I could possibly imagine. He now uses me to train students, who themselves minister to children and youth. I read their essays, in which they confess their own pain and sin. And rather than condemn them and see them as unfit, I am able to disciple them and bring them into the wide-open arms of God's grace.

AMAZING GRACE!

This story has been difficult to tell because it shows my struggle with sin *after* I had been saved. There were certain sins that I thought I would never commit as a Christian. There were certain lines I thought I would never cross. And once I crossed them, I thought there was really nothing left for me. Christians often offer more grace to the unsaved than they do to the saved.

The hymn says, "Amazing grace! How sweet the sound that saved a wretch like me." And we tend to stop with the first verse. We were once saved by grace. Past tense. We were dirty rotten sinners, and Jesus cleaned us up in ways we didn't deserve. Many years ago. And now we're good.

However, we need grace as much today as we did when we first believed. Ongoing grace. Everyday grace. Priceless grace. That we both relish for ourselves and extend to others for the rest of our lives.

A later verse of "Amazing Grace" says it this way:

> *Through many dangers toils and snares*
> *I have already come.*
> *'Tis grace that brought me safe thus far,*
> *And grace will lead me home.*

ACTIONS TO CONSIDER

Watch a movie version of *Les Miserables.*

If someone owes you something, forgive that person the debt.

Then think of a gift you could give that person with no expectation of receiving something in return.

Sing "Amazing Grace" as an act of worship. Then pray and thank God for His grace.

Questions for Reflection and Discussion

- How do you understand grace?
- What is the difference between grace and mercy? (If you need to, look it up.)
- How is your life with God a story of grace?
- In what ways have you received grace recently?

Other Things to Read

Matthew 18

Ephesians 2

Jonathan Aitken, *John Newton: From Disgrace to Amazing Grace* (Crossway).

Victor Hugo, *Les Miserables* (Signet Classics).

Philip Yancey, *What's So Amazing about Grace?* (Zondervan).

#16

SEEK
HEALING

Don't imagine that the trauma of your childhood has been left in the past. It simmers under the surface. And it will surprise you at how suddenly it can boil up or suck you under. The work of healing those hard places might involve reading books or finding counseling. Don't be too afraid or too ashamed to ask for help.

Give sorrow words; the grief that does not speak
whispers the o'er-fraught heart and bids it break.

—WILLIAM SHAKESPEARE, *MACBETH*

Don't let the word "trauma" confuse you or cause you to skip this chapter.

It sounds huge and horrible, and you might imagine that only people who have survived a war or a natural disaster or an act of abuse could claim to suffer its effects.

But that isn't the case. Trauma affects us all.

Dr. Karl Lehman defines "trauma" as any painful experience—

even small or minor—if, as a child, we are without anyone to help us process it appropriately. Lehman says, "The resulting unresolved toxic content carried in the memories for these experiences [can cause] trouble for many years."[1]

Let's break it down.

As we go through childhood and adolescence, we all encounter situations that evoke difficult, negative, painful emotions. Can you think of any of yours? Perhaps our parents left us in the care of someone else for a time, and we felt abandoned. Perhaps another child made fun of us on the playground, and we felt ashamed. Perhaps a sibling seemed to get preferential treatment, and we felt angry. Or perhaps we lost our mother in the mall one day, and we felt afraid.

As children, we do not yet have the emotional intelligence to understand and manage and interpret these feelings on our own. We need the guidance and love of the adults in our lives to get us through unscathed. With their help, we can understand the truth of what happened, and we can learn from it. The pain can heal, and we can grow in wisdom and empathy and relational skills.

However, when healthy processing does not take place—when we are left on our own to deal with it or when our negative feelings are met with ridicule and shame—a painful experience becomes a traumatic one. And the emotions surrounding the incident begin to dig a trench in our brain, a trench that deepens each time that same feeling is unresolved.

These emotional memories aren't like our memories of the day-to-day. We don't picture them or replay them in the same conscious way. Our emotional memories, instead, come into the present more like our memory of learning how to drive. We don't "think" about how to drive.[2] We don't replay our narrative memory about driver's education each time we get behind the wheel. Instead, we just drive.

In a similar way—as we discussed in #12 (Evaluate Your Emotions)—when we encounter a present-day situation that triggers an emotion from our past, our brain automatically runs down that deeply dug trench. We don't think about how or why we feel angry or abandoned or afraid. We don't replay all of the narratives about when we felt that pain before. Instead, we just feel. And because we bring to bear on the present all of the hurt from the past, the feeling is all the more fierce for its history.

IMAGES OF TRAUMA

These narratives sit in our memory like snapshots or a series of stills. When we are triggered and the emotion comes out, our minds don't immediately make the connection between the present and the past. But if we take the time to reflect and relate the two, the resulting revelation will help us heal.

I (Kelli) grew up in a fairly stable family. My parents were compassionate, hardworking, and God-fearing. They stayed married through thick and thin. They kept food on the table and clothes in our closets. They brought my brother and me to church every Sunday and even paid for us to go to private Christian schools. My parents were also physically disabled. They both had cerebral palsy (CP).

In one of my earliest memories from childhood, I am standing in our yard, our big corner lot, out by the street. Second Avenue in Richfield, Minnesota. I am probably three.

I am alone. But I can see my dad and his cane at a distance. Slowly, precariously, he is wobbling down the road. He approaches each modest cookie-cutter house and knocks on the door. He is trying to find me a playmate. My dad was an accountant. He could do math problems in his head. He could have calculated the number of steps he would have to take or the percentage of kids to adults on our street. But this task requires two of the life skills he finds most difficult: walking and talking.

Then it happens. He is halfway down the block, and I see him teeter. I watch him lose his balance. His cane doesn't catch him. And he hits the pavement. Hard. Knees first. Hip. Elbow. Shoulder. I look around for someone to help him. I am not allowed to leave the yard. So I can only watch as he struggles on his own, like a newborn foal, to rise. I feel afraid.

It is traumatic, watching your father fall day after day and seeing the man, who is meant to protect you, lying so vulnerable on the ground.

A few years later, when I am almost six and it is the Fourth of July, I am riding in the backseat of Grandma Eve's yellow Plymouth. We're on our way to celebrate at Uncle Bill's. My mom and brother are beside me. Dad is in the front seat. And Grandma Eve loses control of the car. We swerve violently. Then we roll once and land right-side-up in the ditch. The windows have shattered. And the Tupperware containing Mom's cherry Jell-O has burst open. The red, sugary goop covers my head and torso. Physically, we are only bruised and cut. But Mom is hysterical. Understandably. She thinks I'm a bloody mess.

Passersby stop to help. My dad is crumpled up on the floor under the dash, so a man checks him for injuries, then gently pulls him from the car. A woman yanks my mom's door open, tries to calm her, and helps her out with my toddler brother, who is also crying.

Another stranger comes to me. She takes my hand and guides me over the broken glass. Then she carries me over to her car, away from the scene and away from my family. She washes my face with a rag and removes my sticky shirt. As I hear the

IT IS TRAUMATIC, SEEING THE MOST IMPORTANT MAN IN YOUR LIFE MOCKED SO MERCILESSLY.

emergency vehicles racing to us, I cling—half-naked—to my Jell-O covered doll. I feel alone.

It is traumatic, suffering a car accident and seeing your parents so frantic and being pulled away from everyone familiar when you need them most.

Six years after that, when I am twelve, my parents take me out of the small and safe Lutheran school I have attended since kindergarten. I begin riding a school bus for over an hour each morning to a much bigger Christian school in north Minneapolis. Our bus route takes us by a home for disabled individuals. The residents are often lined up in their wheelchairs outside the front door, or they are pacing up and down on the patio.

One afternoon as our bus passes by that home, a popular high school boy seizes the opportunity to get a laugh. He stumbles down the bus aisle, both hands drawn up in a crippled fashion, his speech slurred, sounding for all the world like my dad. "Look, I'm a spaz!"

The kids on the bus roar with laughter, fueling his performance. And my cheeks burn. I feel angry and ashamed.

It is traumatic, seeing the most important man in your life mocked so mercilessly.

GOING UNDERGROUND

Moments like these are hard for every kid. But, according to Lehman, what makes them truly problematic is when they aren't discussed.[3]

I couldn't (or wouldn't) talk to anyone about the boy on the bus. I couldn't (or wouldn't) talk about how it felt every time my dad fell. I couldn't (or wouldn't) talk about the car accident and the aftermath. Because these incidents were not processed and healed at the time, they seared my soul. They burrowed deep into my brain, and the healing became harder.

For many years afterward—throughout my twenties and beyond—these emotional memories could come flooding back at the drop of a hat. I might respond to an innocent remark by a family member or friend with internal rage. I might react to a breakup with a boy with disproportionate depression. I might lie awake at night feeling isolated and alone to the point of panic. All of it, triggered trauma.

When I (Peter) was in my twenties, the trauma of my child-hood was being triggered as well, though I didn't realize what was happening at the time. I would often feel out of place even though I was popular. I would feel a rush of emotion early in dating relationships that I thought must be love. I would feel deeply rejected if someone had a party and didn't invite me. I assumed these feelings were normal and appropriate. I rode the wave.

Then, in my late twenties when I was teaching in Pakistan, I handled one breakup even worse than I had before. It affected my work since I opted to journal at my desk when I should have been teaching my fifth-grade class. I was trying to shed my pain, but it was too intense. Quite frankly, it was more than the situation warranted, and my boss was watching. She wanted to send me for counseling, but I found that idea humiliating.

GOD WAS LEADING me INTO a JOUrney OF HEALING, anD I HaD TO OBeY.

Instead, I made a decision that seemed like a strong one at the time. Rather than seeking help, I decided to pull myself together and shut down my emotions entirely. My boss praised my turnaround, and I thought I had succeeded.

I no longer kept a journal, I no longer wrote poetry, and I *felt* less. I believed that I was in control, and that my emotions were tamed. I was unaware, however, that I had not healed those emotions. I had only stuffed them and denied them. One day they would burst out with a vengeance.

One day, many years later, I was at work. I was across campus, preparing for a meeting, when a rush of anxiety overcame me. I suddenly felt strongly that I wanted to run back to my office and hide under my desk. It seemed absurd, and I wondered if I were finally losing it. I tried to subdue those strange thoughts in my own strength, but the desire to run away and hide kept intensifying.

I shared the experience with a counselor friend, who suggested that I see a therapist, but I didn't want to. Seeing a counselor would mean admitting failure.

However, I soon sensed God revealing to me that my resistance was pride. He was leading me into a journey of healing, and I had to obey. I made an appointment with a Christian counselor, and what followed was a trail of self-discovery, brokenness, and surrender. The result has been a life of daily dependence on His strength, rather than my own.

HOW HE HEALS US

God wants to heal us from trauma and pain. He is the great Healer. In Exodus 15:26 He revealed Himself to His people as Jehovah-Rapha (The Lord your Healer). In Psalm 103, David praises the Lord, who "who forgives all your iniquity, who heals all your diseases, who redeems your life from the pit, who crowns you with steadfast love and mercy, who satisfies you with good so that your youth is renewed like the eagle's" (vv. 3–5). In Isaiah 53, the prophet tells God's people that "he was pierced for our transgressions" and "crushed for our iniquities" and "by his wounds we are healed" (v. 5 NIV).

ANOTHER PERSON SHARED. AND THEN ANOTHER. AND IN THE END, MY OPENNESS ABOUT MY TRAUMA AND MY JOURNEY OF HEALING LED TO DEEPER FRIENDSHIPS AND OPENED THE DOOR OF HEALING TO OTHERS AS WELL.

God also uses other people to help us heal. The Bible teaches that connectedness and openness are an important part of healing. In Galatians 6:2 Paul tells us to "bear one another's burdens." And James 5:16 says we ought to "confess [our] sins to one another and pray for one another, that [we] may be healed."

After I (Peter) sought counseling, another key decision that I made was to tell my small group of five years what was going on. I knew that I *could* continue to keep my trauma, my weaknesses, and my failings as private as possible. I *could* continue to try to pretend and play the game. Or I could finally open up to them and risk their rejection.

And so one week I shared. Then there was an awkward silence . . . and the meeting ended . . . and I was filled with regret.

The next week, however, another man asked to speak. He had been challenged by my openness and—despite his apparent togetherness—he shared some of his regrets and hurt from the past. Then another person shared. And then another. And in the end, my openness about my trauma and my journey of healing led to deeper friendships and opened the door of healing to others as well.

A few years ago our counselor friend, who had advised Peter to seek help, offered to pray with me (Kelli) as well. She prayed for comfort and clarity and healing. Then we prayed silently for a while. I was skeptical, I admit. But I was also desperate.

It was a pivotal time in my life, and I was in a precarious place. My understanding of trauma had grown over the years. I understood that I was still carrying so much fear and anxiety and shame from my childhood, and I could see how it was affecting much of my present. My marriage. My friendships. My work. My emotional well-being. And even my spiritual life. But I also knew that I couldn't heal myself.

As we sat in Jesus' presence that day, as I begged Him silently to make Himself known, I suddenly saw an image of myself as a little girl—a scared little girl huddled behind a thick brick wall. The little girl whose daddy fell, whose car turned over, whose family was mocked.

Then I saw Him. I envisioned Jesus. A strong, powerful, son-of-a-carpenter Jesus—He came to the wall with a sledgehammer, and with one blow He knocked it right down. Laugh if you like. I did—right out loud in that office.

Then, in my mind's eye, Jesus bent down and offered me His

hand, and I was drawn in by His gentle touch. He pulled me out from behind that demolished wall, and He led me by the hand to a nearby park, where He lifted me onto the swing—like my earthly father never could—and He began to push me. High and free. We played without a care in the world, and His smile was all I could see. He enjoyed me. He cared for me. I was confident of His love. And in that moment, He began to heal many things.

ACTIONS TO CONSIDER

If you think it would be helpful, make plans to see a Christian counselor and talk about your past.

If it is possible, arrange to sit down with one or both of your parents and talk about your childhood. Celebrate the good times and start an open discussion about the hard things.

QUESTIONS FOR REFLECTION AND DISCUSSION

- What experiences from your childhood or adolescence might fall into the category of "trauma" as explained in this chapter?
- Did your parents or other adults help you process painful experiences when you were a child? If so, how? If not, how did you deal with them?
- Can you identify a time recently when you were "triggered" (you responded to a present situation with emotion from the past)? What was the result?
- What might a path of healing look like for you?
- Do you think it would be helpful to talk to someone about your unresolved trauma? A counselor? A parent? A mentor? A small group? A friend? Why or why not? Ask God for wisdom to know if this is the right step.

- What places does Jesus want to heal in your heart? On what truths about Him do you need to meditate?
- How does "trauma"—handled rightly—lead to God?

OTHER THINGS TO READ

Psalm 103

Isaiah 53

Mark 5

Henry Cloud, *Changes That Heal: How to Understand Your Past and Ensure a Healthier Future* (Zondervan).

Karl Lehman, *Outsmarting Yourself: Catching Your Past Invading the Present and What to Do about It* (This Joy! Books).

Sandra D. Wilson, *Released from Shame: Moving Beyond the Pain of the Past* (IVP Books).

#17

LIVE
LOVED

Wake up every morning and—before you put your feet to the floor—let your mind and heart linger on the fact that the Creator of the universe loves you passionately, completely, unconditionally, and eternally. Nothing matters more than this.

> *The Christian does not think God will love us*
> *because we are good, but that God will*
> *make us good because He loves us.*
> —C. S. Lewis

Late one night, a few years ago, Peter and I sat on our tall Craftsman bed in our upstairs bedroom, tucked under the eaves. We were having a hard conversation about love.

I don't remember how it began or what surface issue was at stake, but I do remember that after some time our talk took an unexpected turn.

Something triggered me, and I felt suddenly scared and alone. I remember sobbing into a wad of toilet paper and expressing to Peter a deep and desperate desire to be loved. And I remember Peter patiently laying out for me all the ways he had tried.

Mostly, though, I remember that as I listened to his list—of how he helped around the house and how he took me on dates and how he encouraged me with kind words and many more sacrificial acts—something finally broke through. I realized that, while he had been busy trying to love me, I had been busy building walls. Walls behind which I hid. Walls that prevented me from experiencing much of the love that Peter sent my way. Walls against which his kind acts would crash and shatter. Walls that—even more importantly—kept me from recognizing and fully receiving the love of God.

I hadn't meant to build these walls, of course. They were erected slowly and unconsciously, constructed—brick by brick—with self-reliance and perfectionism and pride. For a long time, my performance-driven self had worked hard to solidify my own sense of worth and to establish an admirable façade. However, I had mistaken accolades and compliments for true affection and care. And I didn't comprehend how praise is unpredictable and fleeting and a very poor substitute for love.

LOVE IS NOT SINGULAR

We all long for love.

We first learn to love from those who love us. Sometimes they do it well. Sometimes not.

We receive love. Enjoy it. Then do our best to pass it on.

We dream of it. Chase after it. Take it for granted when it's ours.

We envy it in others. We miss it when it's gone. And we concoct our own ideas of what it ought to be.

But what is love really?

The movies paint many pictures of love. Sometimes they do it well. Sometimes not. In the 1992 movie *The Last of the Mohicans,* Daniel Day Lewis's character, Hawkeye, has to leave his true love, Cora Munro. They are hidden behind a waterfall in a cave, but their enemies are closing in. Hawkeye wrestles with what to do, but Cora tells him to go, to make his escape. When he decides that he will leave, he implores her with impassioned commitment, "Survive! Stay alive no matter what occurs! I will find you! No matter how long it takes. No matter how far. I will find you!"[1] Of course, the rest of the film shows Hawkeye's pursuit of Cora. If you haven't seen the movie, I'm sure you can guess how it ends.

So is that love?

C. S. Lewis wrote about four kinds of love: *storge* (familial affection), *philia* (friendship), *eros* (passion), and *agape* (spiritual) love.[2] Gary Chapman writes about five love languages: Words of Affirmation, Acts of Service, Receiving Gifts, Quality Time, and Physical Touch.[3]

I (Peter) find both of these books—and even many movies—helpful, and I have come to agree with this premise: love is not a simple or singular thing. Love has many faces and takes many forms. But every time we experience true love in this world, we experience more of God, who is love Himself, after all.

LOVE'S MANY FACES

Each year, at the end of November, the holiday season begins with us bundling Daryl and Amelia and Grandma Viv into the backseat of our SUV and driving six hours north to Minneapolis for Thanksgiving. When we arrive in Excelsior on Lake Minnetonka, it's often late. The children are sleeping, and the grown-ups are feeling close, having taken advantage of the opportunity for extended conversation. Kelli's cousin and her husband greet us warmly. And for a lovely long weekend, we eat delicious food, watch football and movies, and check the paper for Black Friday deals. Aunty Pam reads library books to the kids. Uncle Norm breaks out his guitar, and he and Daryl sing their traditional "Mr. Golden Sun." Norm and Pam's grown children dig out their old toys and welcome Daryl and Amelia to spread them liberally across the wooden floors. We might take in the Macy's Christmas display or the Holidazzle Parade. Or we might not—because what matters most is the familiar fellowship with extended family. By this, we know we are loved.

When Christmas and the New Year come along, we line the floors of our McHenry house with futons. Kelli's brother and his family often come from Tennessee. Friends and former students who have no local family might join us as well. During the day, Kelli's brother Ken fixes broken cabinet doors and crumbling plaster walls, using the tools he brought from Tennessee just for the task. Our teenage nephews and I recruit all other willing souls to play round after round of strategy games. The women chop vegetables and chat over coffee, catching up on all the news. Daryl and Amelia dance and jump and run around the house, proclaiming to anyone who will listen that Christmas is here. The highlight is mealtime, when we all come together around the big table for good food. Turkey and ham, roast potatoes and stuffing, vegetables and cranberries and sausages wrapped in bacon. The conversation roams from topic to topic and carries on through dessert. We are together. We belong. And we know we are loved.

As often as we can, our family gets together with our friends the Skinners. Gary Skinner is also English, so he gets my jokes and my obscure references to British children's television shows. We both think that "football" refers to a sport where you *kick* the ball with your *foot*. And we both support the Liverpool Football Club. Kelli and Kim Skinner help lead our church's adoption ministry together, and they meet up regularly for coffee dates and playdates with the kids. The Skinners' son, Colton, is just about Daryl's age, and the two of them play cars and trucks and trampoline and light sabers. Our families share a common faith and a desire to grow in it, so we formed a small group with the Skinners that met for seven years. The Skinners and the Worralls do a lot of life together. We have grown to love and respect one another because of our shared values and goals.

> Every time we experience true love in this world, we experience more of God, who is love himself.

Most summers I speak at the junior coed week for Lake Geneva Youth Camp in Wisconsin. Some years Kelli comes along and stays the week with me, but some summers she can't. Late one evening, during one of the no-Kelli years, I was alone in my cabin. I had just turned off the main light and was reading by the bedside lamp when there was a knock at my door. Then Kelli burst in. She had been missing me, so she had spontaneously jumped in the car and driven two hours to see me for just a little while that night. In that surprise visit, I saw her passion, and it buoyed my spirits for the rest of the week. I knew I was loved.

One August afternoon several years ago, I stood out in front

> STUDENTS QUICKLY BECOME MORE THAN NAMES ON A LIST, AND WE GET TO KNOW THEM AS INDIVIDUALS WITH UNIQUE GIFTS AND BACKGROUNDS AND DREAMS.

of our old Evanston three-flat. I was digging up dandelions from our sad patch of dirt, and I had stopped to take a rest. An elderly gentleman, who lived in the building next door, approached me and said, "Hello." We started to talk about gardening (a passion of his) and life in Evanston (we were newcomers). Eventually we discovered that the gentleman—Richard—had graduated in 1957 from the school where I was teaching. And our friendship was born. Richard and I started to meet regularly at a local coffee shop to talk about theological and political matters. He would faithfully come with a passage from a book, a cutting from a newspaper, or a report on a television interview he had seen. We became close, but four years later Kelli and I had to move forty miles away to McHenry. Meeting with Richard became much more difficult, but he has demonstrated his love for me and his commitment to our friendship. He visits us in McHenry. He still shares articles with me, but more and more he just listens to my struggles and shares his own. Through my friendship with Richard, I know I am loved.

Every fall, as professors, Kelli and I polish up our courses for a new group of students. On the first day of the semester, we see rows of them, sitting expectantly in our classrooms. We're eager to share what we have for them to learn, but we also worry about disappointing them. Quickly, though, they become more than names on a list, and we get to know them as individuals with unique gifts and backgrounds and dreams. Each year we develop an even deeper connection to and affection for the handful of students who seek us out. They request an appointment or just knock at our office door. Then they settle into the corner chair and tell us their stories. They are vulnerable about how their roommate isn't paying them much attention; they share how their dating relationship is getting serious; or they ask us to share from our own lives what we have learned along the way. When we look into their eyes and see the desire to connect, we feel confirmed in our call. And we relish the opportunity to love our students in ways that we, too, have been loved.

MANY LOVES, ONE GOD

We are not loved in just one way or by just one person. Rather, we are loved in many ways, by many people. And through these many channels, God loves us as well.

We must daily remember this: We are loved by the God of the universe, and we are fortunate to have many tangible reminders.

First, God's love is like the familiar presence of family and friends at the holidays. It's easy to take this love for granted because it doesn't always stir up our emotions. Rather, it is calm and enduring and faithful and noble and sure.

> GOD'S LOVE INVESTS IN US. HE CALLS US TO HIMSELF, AND THEN HE DISCIPLES US ALONG THE WAY.

Second, God loves through His church, through the community of believers, who share our interests, aims, and mission. He grows our love for one another as we pursue our common goal of living fully for Him. He shares Himself with us too—through Jesus, who knows our burdens and our pain. Jesus, like us, was thirsty and hungry and needed to rest. Jesus, like us, had His own community of friends He loved and who loved Him.

Third, God loves us with passion. He burns with a desire for us to know Him. He covers the vast expanse between heaven and earth to be with us. He has redeemed us and reconciled us to Himself, so that Paul says, "For I am sure that neither death nor life, nor angels nor rulers, nor things present nor things to come, nor powers, nor height nor depth, nor anything else in all creation, will be able to separate us from the love of God in Christ Jesus our Lord" (Romans 8:38–39).

In effect He says, in the words of Hawkeye, "I will come for you!"

Finally, God's love invests in us. He calls us to Himself, and then He disciples us along the way. He breathes life into us. He comforts us. He teaches us. He listens to us. He disciplines us. And He feeds our soul.

THE STORY OF LAZARUS ON LOVE

I (Kelli) have directed your attention to the story of Lazarus a couple of times already. There is still much for us to glean. I want to take us there one more time because John 11 actually opens with multiple declarations of *love*. Lazarus's sisters, Mary and Martha, send a message to Jesus. "The one whom you *love* is sick." And in case we didn't get it, two verses later John explains that Jesus *loves* them all—Lazarus and Mary and Martha too. They are the best of friends, like family even.

But as we saw in #8 (Be Patient), though Jesus loves them, He does not hurry to their side when He hears that Lazarus is sick.

Instead, He stays where He is for a full two days. We might wonder why. Certainly, Mary and Martha do. "If you had been here," they both tell Jesus when He finally does arrive, "our brother wouldn't have died."

But John makes it clear why Jesus decided to delay. He wasn't lazy or dismissive or disinterested or cruel. It was for the glory of God; Jesus said so Himself. It was so that they might believe.

When Jesus finally comes into town, Mary and Martha are mourning, and again we are assured of Jesus' love for them because He weeps too. Then He says, "Remove the stone."

In spite of her desire to see her brother alive again, Martha protests. "By this time he will stink."

Then Jesus looks her in the eye, and He says, "Did I not tell you that if you believed you would see the glory of God?" (v. 40). Then He prays aloud and shouts into the tomb, "Lazarus, come out!" And the dead man walks.

We always, *always* get Jesus' love—a love that comes to us in good time, a love that weeps with us, and a love that shouts into our darkest places and calls forth new life.

This story shows us so much about how Jesus loves. It shows us that He doesn't always act in the way we'd like. He doesn't always hurry to our aid when we call. Rather, He perfectly times His loving deeds to bring about the glory of God and our belief.

We must also understand that although we don't always get the Lazarus ending, we always, *always* get Jesus' love—a love that comes to us in good time, a love that weeps with us, and a love that shouts into our darkest places and calls forth new life.

ACTIONS TO CONSIDER

Take the "How We Love" love style quiz at howwelove.com. Share your results with someone close to you.

QUESTIONS FOR REFLECTION AND DISCUSSION

- What false ideas about love have seeped into your thinking?
- When have you been truly loved?
- How have you experienced the *storge* love (familial affection)?
- How have you experienced *eros* (passion) love?
- How does God show His love to you?

OTHER THINGS TO READ AND BROWSE

John 11

1 Corinthians 12–14

1 John 1

Gary Chapman, *The 5 Love Languages* (Northfield); www.5lovelanguages.com.

C. S. Lewis, *The Four Loves* (Harcourt).

C. S. Lewis, *Till We Have Faces* (Harcourt).

18

CULTIVATE AN ETERNAL PERSPECTIVE

Train your eyes on this hope, this inheritance, that will "never perish, spoil or fade." That is "kept in heaven for you." For it is in this that you are "filled with an inexpressible and glorious joy" (1 Peter 1:4, 8 NIV). Peter (the apostle) said it better than we ever could. Here's just a sampling.

WHAT A GOD WE HAVE!

And how fortunate we are to have him, this Father of our Master Jesus! Because Jesus was raised from the dead, we've been given a brand-new life and have everything to live for, including a future in heaven—and the future starts now! God is keeping careful watch over us and the future. The Day is coming when you'll have it all—life healed and whole.

—1 PETER 1:3–5 (MSG)

Yesterday I (Peter) took the train home from work—from Chicago to McHenry—a 75-minute ride, during which I relaxed and released the stress of the day. I also reflected on my teaching—the classroom discussions about discipleship and worldview, the private office conversations about Jesus' healing power. And as I traveled home, my mind was set on these things from above.

When my train arrived at the McHenry station, Kelli was waiting for me. She was sitting in our car, looking happy to see me. I climbed into the passenger seat, smiled, gave her a kiss. Then I asked her how her day had been.

"Well," she said, with the telling sigh I know so well, "I took the car to have the battery changed, but it's still not right."

Earlier in the week we had taken this same car to the dealership for some very expensive suspension work. But after the "repairs" had been made, the suspension was still giving us trouble. As if that weren't irritating enough—on the drive home from the shop that afternoon, multiple new warning lights had come on. They mocked us from the dash. When I had called the dealership to report the situation, their mechanic expressed confidence that the suspension was fine, and he suggested that a new battery should deal with the lights.

However, as Kelli informed me last night, the new battery didn't fix the problem, the warning lights were still glaring at us, and the car was going to have to go back to the shop for the third time this week. My frustration mounted quickly. And just like that, the cares of this world captured my attention and pulled my focus from the eternal—and back to the here and now.

As we drove home from the train station, Kelli and I began to discuss whether she should take the car back in on Thursday or whether I should take it on Friday. If Kelli accepted the task, she would lose valuable time that she needed to work on this book. But if I did it, I would lose time that I needed to work on a doctoral paper that had to be submitted within the week. Back and forth we went until at some point, we both groaned, "We don't have time for this."

BOUND BY TIME

Time can be an uncomfortable companion and an ill-fitted friend. How often our to-do list expands beyond the capacity of our ticking clock and our calendar pages. How often we feel time pressing in on us. How often we try to grab at its heels as it scurries away—always just out of reach.

In one breath, we might beg time to move more quickly. We want to hurry the hands on the big clock face and rush to a reunion or a celebration or a longed-for life event. But when we arrive at these occasions, we sometimes seek to stop time in its tracks—to grab it with both hands and squeeze it tight.

We are rarely completely contented in its hourglass form. We are rarely in comfortable sync with the sands as they flow through the shaft.

But if our human existence on this planet is constrained by time—by the spinning of our globe and by the rising and setting of our sun—it is also constrained by space.

CONSTRAINED BY SPACE

We inhabit this world in a limited physical form. We take in the universe through the same five senses that human beings have used since time began. We live and move in a body that smells a wood fire in the air, that feels both the sting of a bee and a warm embrace. A body that tastes a creamy Cadbury chocolate bar and also hears the sirens of emergency vehicles racing to a tragic scene.

This body brings with it needs and desires that demand to be filled on a daily basis. Needs and desires that are sometimes subtle, other times overpowering; sometimes simple, more often complex—sometimes even contradictory. Certainly, we need food and water and air to breathe. But while we long for the sense of well-being that a healthy meal will bring, we also crave the salsa and tortilla chips in the cupboard and have to stop ourselves before we eat the whole bag. While we want the safety of our steady, full-time administrative job, we also hunger for the adventure and fulfillment we imagine could be found if we followed our artistic dreams. While we long for proximity and community with other human beings, we also—simultaneously—desire a space to call our own.

When I arrived at home last night, I knew I had to phone the dealership—yet again—before they closed for the evening. I went into the empty living room, sat on the sofa, gathered my wits, called the dealership, and waited for the operator to put me through to the service crew.

Kelli was distracted, making dinner, so just as I was connected to the appropriate representative, Daryl and Amelia came screaming into the room. I motioned for them to go back to the kitchen, but Daryl was undeterred. He climbed up on

GOD HAD DISAPPEARED IN THE DETAILS—OF CARS AND CHILDREN. OF TERRESTRIAL TIME AND SPACE.

the sofa, launched himself into the air, and landed on me with a thud. Unwittingly, I let out a loud, "Ugh!" right into the phone.

As I grabbed Daryl's arm and ushered him from the room, I apologized to the woman on the other end of the line for grunting at her. With the phone still to my ear, I appeared angrily in the kitchen, hoping that my frustrated nonverbals would send a clear message. I needed quiet, and I needed space.

I carried the tension of that whole exchange through dinner, missing the chance to interact with my family in any eternally significant way. It wasn't until much later—when Kelli was putting the kids to bed—that my mind and heart softened to what I had lost. And I realized that, for much of our evening, God had disappeared in the details—of cars and children. Of terrestrial time and space.

But last night wasn't an isolated incident. It wasn't even a particularly poignant example of how to pursue an eternal perspective. For several hours, I lost the plot. But this narrative does demonstrate the perpetual pull of the things of this world. It illustrates the ease with which we can be derailed and distracted by the daily details. And it serves as a reminder that—despite the reality of broken cars and noisy kids and a myriad of minutiae that fight for our focus—we are much more than terrestrial beings. And our existence matters more than such trivialities might lead us to believe.

PETER, PAUL, AND PLATO

In his work *The Republic,* the Greek philosopher Plato (approx. 427–347 B.C.) presents "The Allegory of the Cave." It is written as a dialogue—between Plato's brother Glaucon and his mentor Socrates—in which Socrates describes a group of people who have been chained to the wall of a cave for their entire life. Their legs and their necks are secured in such a way that they are forced to stare at a blank wall. Behind them is a fire. Also behind them, but in front of the fire, are people carrying puppets—puppets of still other men and living things. The puppets project shadows on the bare wall. And as the prisoners watch the shadows come and go, they begin to assign names and meaning to the images. For the prisoners, this is their only understanding of reality.

Plato then likens a philosopher to a prisoner who is freed from the cave. Only with this release, only with the exchange of sunlight for firelight, can one come to understand the true nature of reality, says Plato. Only then can one rise above the evidence of the senses to the greater truths in the world of the mind.

The biblical writers of the New Testament wrote in Greek. They knew Greek culture and were influenced by it. Paul, in particular, was ideally positioned for ministry with Jews and non-Jews because he had studied widely and was educated in both Jewish and Greek culture. In his letters to the Philippians and Colossians, we see what might be echoes of Plato. Paul acknowledges that we should pay attention to the realities around us—the needs of our physical being. But he cautions us against a form of idolatry that makes such needs supreme. He argues, instead, that these physical realities must lead us to an eternal perspective. Look at Philippians 3, for example. In verses 17–21 (NIV) Paul writes:

> Join together in following my example, brothers and sisters, and just as you have us as a model, keep your eyes on those who live as we do. For, as I have often told you before and

now tell you again even with tears, many live as enemies of the cross of Christ. Their destiny is destruction, their god is their stomach, and their glory is in their shame. Their mind is set on earthly things. But our citizenship is in heaven. And we eagerly await a Savior from there, the Lord Jesus Christ, who, by the power that enables him to bring everything under his control, will transform our lowly bodies so that they will be like his glorious body.

Think of this passage in the light of what Paul likely learned from both Greek and Jewish culture. He tells the Philippians to use their eyes, to look at the examples of his life and those around him. Paul's life stands in contrast to the many around him who are focused on satiating their five senses—as if this world was all that there is. Paul urges the Philippians—and us— to not set our minds on satisfying our physical desires. He tells the Philippians—and us—to not live primarily as citizens of this world, not primarily as citizens of the United States with its rampant consumerism, not primarily as citizens of the European Union with its godless hedonism. Paul urges us instead to live primarily as citizens of heaven. Heaven's citizens enjoy their food and drink of this earthly realm, but in their proper place, as they anticipate the day when this mundane existence will be transformed into something glorious that we will need new and glorious bodies to contain. When our Savior comes and leads us home, the life we were meant to live will be fully revealed.

Cultivating an eternal perspective was so important to Paul that he wrote of it again in his letter to the Colossians. Consider Colossians 2:16–19:

Therefore let no one pass judgment on you in questions of food and drink, or with regard to a festival or a new moon or a Sabbath. These are a shadow of the things to come, but the substance belongs to Christ. Let no one disqualify you, insisting on asceticism and worship of angels, going on in detail about visions, puffed up without reason by his sensuous mind, and not holding fast to the Head, from whom the whole body, nourished and knit together through its joints and ligaments, grows with a growth that is from God.

The Colossians were writing each other off, based on their behavior. They insisted on adherence to the Jewish laws. I didn't grow up under the Jewish law, but I knew another form of legalism. I knew that I would be harshly judged by some in my church if I kicked a soccer ball around on a Sunday. Every Saturday night all balls were safely locked away lest anyone be enticed into a sinful Sunday scrimmage. Paul acknowledges that rules do have their place, but the Old Testament laws were intended to point to something greater. Paul even uses Plato's language to explain that the reality of the day-to-day should lead us to contemplate the eternal reality, the greatest of which is the mystery of Jesus Christ.

CULTIVATING an eternal perspective means paying attention to the nagging ache in our soul, the tug that tells us that we were meant for more than this.

In Colossians chapter 3 Paul continues the theme. There he tells the Colossians as clear as can be to focus on things above, not on earthly things. He does not suggest, as some cults try to tell us, that earthly things do not exist or do not matter. Their importance, though, is not in and of themselves. The earthly things that God has created point beyond themselves. They point above, and that is where our focus ought to be.

But what does that look like in the day-to-day?

In that moment last night—with the car and the phone call and the crazy household—it meant remembering that, in God's eyes, my time here on earth becomes but a blip. What to me looks so big, to Him seems so small.

But it means more than that as well.

Cultivating an eternal perspective means paying attention to the nagging ache in our soul, the tug that tells us that we were meant for more than this. It means accepting that this life will never completely satisfy because our existence here is only part of the story. As the philosopher in Ecclesiastes says, "He has put eternity into man's heart, yet so that he cannot find out what God has done from the beginning to the end" (Ecclesiastes 3:11).

Cultivating an eternal perspective means setting our sights on what lies beyond—not only on what lies before. When we savor good food, we anticipate even more the bountiful banquet we will one day enjoy, seated at God's eternal table, unashamed (Matthew 22:2). When we sing with the saints for His sake, we add our voices to the heavenly throng, crying "Holy, holy, holy, is the Lord God Almighty!" (Revelation 4:8). When we gaze at the natural world, we also see through it to the One who transcends His creation. When we don't have enough time, we yearn for eternity. When we don't have enough space, we contemplate the vastness of the universe and the enormity of our God.

Cultivating an eternal perspective means holding on to our fixed and future hope, as Peter (the apostle) proclaims. A hope that can only result from Jesus' resurrection from the dead and the new life that He alone can give. A hope that provides joy in times of trials and power in times of fear. A hope that see its future in heaven not as a distant ideal, but as a present reality. A hope that is defined as an inheritance—everlasting and incorruptible and pure. A hope that comes from faith and results in praise (1 Peter 1:3–9).

Actions to consider

Watch Louie Giglio's talk online: "Mashup of Stars and Whales Singing God's Praise." Ponder the vastness of God's universe.

Spend a whole day (probably not a workday) without checking the time. Leave your watch and your phone at home. Discuss your observations with a friend.

Visit a planetarium. Contemplate the vastness of space.

Questions for reflection and discussion

- How often do you look beyond time and space to eternity?
- What prevents you from cultivating an eternal perspective?
- What happens when you stop, let go of the details of the day to day, and spend time focusing outside of yourself? What changes when you contemplate that our existence here on this earth is not all that there is?
- Where in your life do you have the opportunity to make an eternal difference? How could you cultivate more of these opportunities?

OTHER THINGS TO READ

Philippians 3

Colossians 2 and 3

1 Peter 1

Francis Chan, *Crazy Love: Overwhelmed by a Relentless God* (David C. Cook).

19

MAKE GOD'S GLORY YOUR GOAL

I (Kelli) used to repeatedly recite the following mantra to myself when a big project loomed and I feared the outcome. Would I succeed or fail? Would my reputation rise or fall? "It's not about me. It's all about Him." I said it over and over and over again. I still do. And I am confident in this: He will do whatever brings Him glory. That is all that matters. That is all I desire. Remembering this removes all of the pressure.

For what we proclaim is not ourselves,
but Jesus Christ as Lord.

—2 Corinthians 4:5

Pride. It's the oldest sin in the book, and perhaps the most pervasive.

We learn from Isaiah 14 that pride was at the core of Satan's fall. He believed he could ascend to heaven and establish his own throne above the throne of God. When that scheme ended badly, the serpent tried to tempt Eve with a similar delusion, telling her, "You will not surely die. For God knows that when you eat of it your eyes will be opened, and you will be like God, knowing good and evil" (Genesis 3:4–5). She liked the look of the fruit and the promise of wisdom. So she bought the lie, and she ate. Adam did too. And ever since then, Satan attempts to deceive each and every one of us in like manner.

So we must war.

We war with him—that prowling lion (1 Peter 5:8). We war with "our flesh"—that daily sets its desires up against the Spirit (Galatians 5:17). And we war with our pride—with all of its faces and forms: jealousy, idolatry, self-reliance, greed, timidity, aggression, lust, and shame (Galatians 5:19–21).

We war every day in multiple ways. Some attacks come at us double-barreled. Some attacks happen in stealth. Regardless, we do not struggle alone. We have an almighty Advocate and Army Commander, who sometimes holds the line Himself and gives us a chance to escape. Other times He calls us to take up our sword, to lift up our eyes from the fight, and to focus on His Son, the founder of our faith, where we can find the strength to endure and the power to overcome (Hebrews 12:1–2).

ZOMBIES

I (Peter) always like a war analogy, but I think zombies might also help us here. Hang with me for a second.

Zombies are fleshy and rotten and worm-eaten, right? They pop up when you least expect them. And if they get a chance, they will eat your brain. Beware. For those of us who know Jesus, our old nature, our flesh, our sin, is a bit like that. A zombie, who wants to take over and destroy our life. This is the substance of our former self. It's a dead self that is not truly us and wants to do us harm.

Some "zombies" are very obviously awful. Those of us who have indulged in certain destructive activities know this only too well. Those of us who have bought into some of Satan's lies can't deny the corrosive consequences because they are on undisputable display. A heroin addiction reduces us to just a shadow of our former selves. Indiscriminate sex can leave us with an STD. A violent temper leaves its target—and perhaps some innocent bystanders—lying critically injured in its wake.

However, other "zombies" can go for a long time undetected. They masquerade in makeup. They dress up in a skirt or a suit, and we fail to see just how much they stink. Such is the zombie of pride. It can look so good. It can be so seductive. It sometimes serves so sacrificially. It leads so dynamically. It masquerades as love and light. But it ultimately sucks our focus into ourselves.

ROGER V. THE ZOMBIES

Certainly Kelli and I have fought with our own zombie pride and will continue to do so. It doesn't die easily or entirely. It keeps coming back to life. We've also talked with many others—friends and students—whose zombie pride is gaining control. Sometimes they see past its clever costume. Other times they don't.

My friend and former student Roger comes to mind.

Roger grew up in a home that called itself "Christian." His parents took him to church and insisted that Roger have a relationship with God. However, when they gave up on their own relationship and divorced when Roger was young, he was left stunned and devastated.

Roger gave his life to Jesus when he was a child. And although his initial commitment was sincere, as time went on, his faith became primarily about performance. He played the Christian game, and he played it well. He shared his faith with family and friends. He knew his Bible inside and out. He would give his last dollar to help a person in need. He was pleasant and people-pleasing. Over the years Roger constructed an elaborate, super-Christian façade—so elaborate that it seemed real, even to him.

However, unbeknownst to him, Roger was living out a deal. Deep down Roger believed that if he dedicated himself to the service of God, God would deliver the security and fulfillment that he desperately desired, but never had.

I had known Roger for about three years when the super-Christian façade began to crack.

A clear crevice occurred when Roger took stock of his life— his dating experiences, work and social opportunities, and emotional well-being. The rewards that Roger had long expected for his good behavior were not being delivered. And when Roger realized that God was not playing by his rules, Roger got mad. He decided that God was withholding things from him. In fact, he wasn't even sure there was a God anymore. But if there was, He wasn't fair, and He certainly wasn't good.

THE BUSY CHRISTIAN ACTIVITY WAS REPLACED BY CONTEMPLATION AND CONFESSION.

To distract himself from his disappointment with God and to fulfill the longing he had for love, Roger threw himself into another dating relationship that became overly physical. For some time, Roger vacillated between committing and running away. Eventually, he broke it off because he couldn't handle the duplicity.

Lying wounded on the ground, Roger finally began to see his false religious façade for what it was. A mask of pride. A life lived for self. And he began to acknowledge the fleshy zombie that lived beneath—that angry, desperate creature. Both selves needed to be slain.

As we met, week after week, I saw Roger become more and more authentic with God and more fervent in his desire to know Him. The busy Christian activity was replaced by contemplation and confession. Roger had to acknowledge that—although he had been a Christian for years—he had fed a false faith. He had sought his own comfort and reputation. Now he had to go back to the basics. Roger had to put to death his pride and become a child again.

Roger still struggles, as we all do. His life sometimes looks like three steps forward and two steps back. But God often breaks through in pretty big ways. Now when Roger wanders, God is more easily able to bring him back, and Roger gives Him the glory because it's all about Him anyhow.

A War Cry

We do this by keeping our eyes on Jesus,
the champion who initiates and perfects our faith.
Because of the joy awaiting him, he endured the cross,
disregarding its shame. Now he is seated in the place
of honor beside God's throne.

—HEBREWS 12:2 (NLT)

Kelli and I married in an old Anglican church in my hometown of Plympton, England. Sections of St. Mary's church date back to the Middle Ages. The stained glass windows and the solid stone pillars certainly added majesty to the occasion. The pews were filled with our family and friends—the men in suits and ties, the women in their hats.

However, I wasn't focused on the church or the crowd that day. Their beauty and glory paled in comparison to that of my bride—because she meant more to me than the location or the crowd. And she was standing by my side, pledging to me her life.

Beyond my bride, though, I was ultimately focused on the One whom I want to fill all of my vision for all of my days. As a part of our ceremony, I requested that we sing the timeless hymn "Be Thou My Vision." It was the anthem of our wedding day. It has been a refocusing refrain for our marriage. And I pray that it would be a rally cry for all of our lives. To God alone be the glory.

> *Be Thou my Vision, O Lord of my heart;*
> *Naught be all else to me, save that Thou art.*
> *Thou my best Thought, by day or by night,*
> *Waking or sleeping, Thy presence my light.*
> *Be Thou my Wisdom, and Thou my true Word;*
> *I ever with Thee and Thou with me, Lord;*
> *Thou my great Father, I Thy true son;*
> *Thou in me dwelling, and I with Thee one.*
> *Be Thou my battle Shield, Sword for the fight;*
> *Be Thou my Dignity, Thou my Delight;*
> *Thou my soul's Shelter, Thou my high Tower:*
> *Raise Thou me heavenward, O Power of my power.*
> *Riches I heed not, nor man's empty praise,*

Thou mine Inheritance, now and always:
Thou and Thou only, first in my heart,
High King of Heaven, my Treasure Thou art.
High King of Heaven, my victory won,
May I reach Heaven's joys, O bright Heaven's Sun!
Heart of my own heart, whatever befall,
Still be my Vision, O Ruler of all.

ACTIONS TO CONSIDER

Listen to "Be Thou My Vision" and sing it through.

Make a list of your life goals. Evaluate if each one is being lived out by your true self which glorifies God or the zombie (flesh) self which lives for itself.

QUESTIONS FOR REFLECTION AND DISCUSSION

- If the true self lives for God, and the zombie (flesh) self doesn't, which self is winning in your life right now? Why?
- Are you horrified at the version of yourself that lives for self?
- How does this chapter integrate with #14 (Take Sin Seriously)?
- In what ways is God leading you to crucify the flesh and commit to Him? Does He want you to sit in silence? Is there something that you're not doing? How can you trust God to live for Him more fully?

OTHER THINGS TO READ

Exodus 20

Andrew Murray, *Abide in Christ* (Trinity Press).

#20

FINALLY, PREPARE TO BE AMAZED

Your life may look something like you envisioned, or it may take you to places that you never imagined. Regardless, hold on tight, because God is in the business of blowing your mind.

I am the LORD, your Holy One, Israel's Creator and King.
I am the LORD, who opened a way through the waters,
making a dry path through the sea. I called forth the
mighty army of Egypt with all its chariots and horses.
I drew them beneath the waves, and they drowned,
their lives snuffed out like a smoldering candlewick. But
forget all that—it is nothing compared to what I am
going to do. For I am about to do something new. See,
I have already begun! Do you not see it?

—ISAIAH 43:15–19 (NLT)

Tuesday is the day of the week that Emily Freeman likes to call the most ordinary one. Today is Tuesday. And in some ways this Tuesday feels just like that—ordinary.

I (Kelli) am sitting at our ordinary ol' dining room table, sipping an ordinary ol' cup of tea. The oniony smell of potato leek soup wafts in from the slow cooker in the kitchen—a recipe I've made dozens of times. The dust mop leans against the wall—a reminder of the ordinary tasks I have yet to do this afternoon. An ordinary stuffed puppy and toy airplane lie forgotten on the floor. The kids—to whom the puppy and the plane belong—are at school. Peter is at work. And I have the house to myself for these few ordinary hours.

A slushy, icy snow is falling outside my windows. This is unfortunately ordinary—and rather irritating—for early March in the Chicagoland area. I can hear the scrape of our neighbor's shovel as he pointlessly tries to clear his walk in the middle of the storm. (I, on the other hand, have wisely decided to let the slop accumulate and freeze on our driveway until Peter gets home.)

But for all of its ordinary elements, this Tuesday—in other ways—feels anything but.

This Tuesday I am attempting to write this—the final chapter of our first book. There's nothing ordinary about that, right? The manuscript is due to the publisher in T-minus twenty days. So the pressure is on, and I feel absolutely inadequate for the task.

See, this book has been a bit of a battle.

Not a battle between Peter and me. (Thank You, Lord.) By the grace and guidance of God alone, we've enjoyed tackling this task together. It's stretched us and opened our eyes. We've seen Him once again use our individual—and very different—strengths in complementary ways. We've learned to listen to each other on a new level. And I think that Peter will agree (I'll ask him tonight after he finishes hacking through that layer of ice) that we are closer now than we were before we began.

No, the fight for this book has been something other than that. Something more and something multifaceted. It has resided sometimes in the physical realm. I've had trouble sleeping, and Peter's been perpetually sick. We've had random, repeated, major repairs to our cars and to our house. The worst of this happened just two Tuesdays ago when I came home to find three *extraordinary* waterfalls running

Sometimes God will turn our biggest struggles and disappointments in life into the greatest demonstrations of His glory and love.

from our kitchen ceiling and then down to the basement. The toilet in our upstairs bathroom had spontaneously decided to overflow—for seven hours straight. The plumber couldn't figure out why. Our old wooden kitchen floor was damaged. Some walls will need repair. The carpet and ceiling in the basement are significantly stained. And our insurance company estimates at least $11,000 of work.

It's been an emotional battle as well—and, most significantly, a spiritual one. Sometimes brutal. Peter and I have both wrestled with discouragement and fear and self-doubt. While God has repeatedly confirmed to us His call, the enemy has seemingly gone out of his way to give us grief. But it's forced us—yet again—into a deep and daily dependence. Right where we ought to be.

Why do I tell you this? For several reasons really. Because you will undoubtedly experience a similar sort of battle. Perhaps you already have. Perhaps you are even now in the midst of one. Because sometimes when God calls us, when He moves us and seeks to use us, sometimes when He is preparing to display His power in profound ways, all we can see with our physical eyes is the opposing army closing in from behind and the waves of the sea stretching out in front. Because sometimes God will turn our biggest struggles and disappointments in life into the greatest demonstrations of His glory and love.

I tell you this, too, because we believe God can do something new—in and through this generation. In fact, we believe He has already begun.

OUR AMAZING GOD

How do we know?

Because of who He is.

Last Thursday—while our house was still a mess from the toilet flood—I flew off to Austin, Texas, for a conference. I considered cancelling the trip. I didn't think I had the time to spare or the energy to devote. But in the end, I went in faith that God would meet me there—tired and distracted as I was. And He did.

He showed up—big time—in the very first session when Mary DeMuth spoke from Isaiah chapter 43. An unusual choice, I thought. But it was exactly the reminder I needed—of who our God is and what He is about. You can read a few verses from Isaiah 43 above. But have a look at the whole chapter when you can. Of course, the original recipient of these promises was the nation of Israel. But our God has not changed. His power has not diminished. Nor has He abandoned His persistent pursuit of His people.

As He did for Israel in Isaiah 43, even now He calls *us* His own and addresses *us* by name. Even now He promises His presence when the waters are deep and the rivers run high and the fires of oppression threaten to consume. Even now He finds *us* precious and lavishes on us His love. Even now He asks *us* to trust—and not fear—because He alone is God. Even now He saves us and proclaims His salvation to the entire world. Even now He invites *us* to be His witnesses. Even now.

And as we anticipate His work in the present, as we prepare to be amazed yet again, it is—even now—a helpful and important practice to remind ourselves—as Isaiah reminded Israel—of all He has done in the *past*.

A QUICK TRIP THROUGH HISTORY

Of course, we could cite innumerable examples from history—biblical history, church history, and our own family history as well. Examples of how God has captured the attention of His children and dropped their jaws and filled their hearts with gratitude beyond belief. We could cite examples both flashy and ordinary, because sometimes we stand amazed when God answers our prayers in exactly the way we asked. Sometimes we stand amazed when He does something completely unexpected and beyond belief. But sometimes we stand amazed simply when He provides a moment of shade in the middle of the desert. Sometimes His power looks like spontaneous combustion, but sometimes—many times—it looks like a slow and steady burn. We can certainly stand amazed when He makes a mighty path through the sea. But we can also stand amazed each and every Tuesday—simply because He is.

In addition to the parting of the sea and Isaiah 43, we could point to so many other stories in His Word. From the Old Testament, we could recall the crumbling of the Jericho wall and Daniel's protection in the lions' den. We could consider the miracles of His Son, Jesus Christ, walking on water and feeding five thousand with just two loaves of bread and a handful of fish. We could watch as Jesus called the little children to Himself, healed the leper, and raised Lazarus from the dead. Then we could stand at the foot of His cross. We could marvel at His sacrifice on our behalf. We could mourn with His mother and the other disciples. And on the third day we could follow Mary Magdalene and the other Mary to the tomb. We could gaze into that empty grave, and we may stand amazed.

We could look to church history, too, and stand amazed at the preservation of the body of Christ—against all odds. As just one example, we could look to fourteenth-century Europe, threatened for decades by the bubonic plague and the Ottoman Turks and the deep corruption in the Roman Catholic Church. Then, from the centuries that followed, we could remember anew the timely invention of Johannes Gutenberg's press and the courage of one obscure monk named Martin Luther, who stood for biblical truth and initiated widespread and long-lasting reform.

> We could cite innumerable examples of how God has captured the attention of His children and dropped their jaws and filled their hearts with gratitude beyond belief.

We could look back at America's very early days. The first settlers from England and Europe arrived, at least in part, with a missionary zeal and a desire for freedom of worship. But by the early eighteenth century, the evangelistic enthusiasm of the pioneering generation had diminished. An increase in wealth and comfort had fostered widespread materialism and a settling for simple moralism in the church. Enter Jonathan Edwards, philosopher and theologian and pastor of the Congregational church in Northampton, Massachusetts. In 1733 God used his series of sermons on justification by faith to spark a revival which spread throughout New England and even over to Wales and England and Europe. England and Wales then sent preachers like Whitefield and Wesley back to America. We know this now as the Great Awakening, and we still stand amazed.

We could look to the lives of so many missionaries and martyrs over the centuries—from William Tyndale to Hudson Taylor to Gladys Aylward to Jim and Elisabeth Elliot to the countless Christians even today who cling to their faith in the face of persecution. We could commend their commitment, of course. But mostly we stand amazed at what God will do through a life wholly devoted to Him (2 Chronicles 16:9).

We *could* simply take a look around us, for within our own sphere of friends and students and acquaintances are innumerable and incredible stories of God's power to seek and to save. We could tell you about Thomas, who was dramatically rescued from addiction, and who now ministers to others, encouraging them to seek the same release that he has received. We could tell you about Tyler, whose fractured relationship with his parents has been slowly, but nonetheless miraculously, restored. We could tell you about Kathy, whom God is healing from a history of horrific abuse. We could tell you about Janelle, who tragically lost her child and then her marriage—who experienced pain far beyond her capacity to cope. But if you talked to Janelle today, she would tell you about the strong arms of her God that wrapped around her and held her tight while she cried. She would tell you about His healing touch and His sustaining power. She would proclaim His goodness and grace. And you would stand amazed at how God has used her faith to call many to Himself.

And finally, we *could* tell you some stories of our own. Both flashy and ordinary—about how God has captured our attention and dropped our jaws and filled our hearts with gratitude beyond belief.

AMAZED BY ADOPTION

I (Kelli) already told you about my first overseas missions trip when I was twenty-two. This was the trip where God opened an unexpected door for me to serve Him in Romania, the one where He blew my mind in many memorable ways.

I also told you, in those early pages, about meeting Peter. I mentioned how I spent the whole of my twenties enduring difficult dating relationships, painful breakups, and long nights of loneliness. I told you about meeting Peter when I was twenty-nine. And I remain amazed—at how God brought us together, sustained our marriage through turbulent times, continues to grow us, and still chooses to use us in spite of ourselves.

I also told you about my decade of longing to be a mom. (Our Story and #13: Press into Pain.) I told you a little bit about the pain of infertility and miscarriages and failed adoptions, about my depression and anger and despair.

What you don't know yet is how our son, Daryl, came to us unexpectedly one March. How we held our breath as his case wound through the foster courts at a sometime snail's pace and

We all stood amazed—at that divine detail, at how God had brought us through six years of pain, six years of waiting.

we waited—with our red raw hearts in our hands—to see what God would do.

I told you how we started the China adoption process three years before we met Daryl and that our two-year wait turned into six. You can imagine how we wondered if our daughter would ever come.

But what you don't know yet is this. One January evening, we finally saw her picture. We finally received our referral, and we began to watch unfold what God had been planning all along. A few weeks later we received our US embassy appointment. That all-important date. The final step in our six-year adoption journey. That was the day we would visit the embassy in Guangzhou with Amelia and receive her American passport. Finally, we would be able to bring her home. The date we were given for that appointment was March 26.

Just days after that appointment letter arrived, we traveled by train to a courtroom in Chicago to petition for Daryl's adoption as well. Peter and I and Daryl and Peter's mum all stood in a silent line in front of the judge while our attorney presented the papers to him. He reviewed the case and asked a few questions. Then he wrote his recommendation and told us, "You don't have to be present, but the court will finalize your adoption of Daryl on March 26."

I turned to Peter and Mum right there in the courtroom, with jaw dropped and eyes wide and mind blown, and said, "That's the same exact day that we'll be finalizing everything in China." And we all stood amazed—at that divine detail, at how God had brought us through six years of pain, six years of waiting. We stood amazed at how He had blessed us in spite of our sometimes fickle faith.

AMAZING ADVENTURE

I (Peter) could tell you a story or two myself.

I might start with London. One late spring, when I was eighteen, I was working for London City Mission, and I needed to catch a bus back to Plymouth, my hometown in the southwest. I can't remember why I was delayed, but I missed the last bus of the night. Feeling dejected I tried to think of a place to sleep, and I decided to head to Victoria train station.

As I sat on the cold stone floor and tried to get warm by curling into a ball, I started to talk to a young man from Glasgow who had also missed his connection and had nothing better to do than sit and wait to leave the next day. With mission on my mind, I soon pressed into the existence of God and the gospel message. Before the police moved us on just before sunrise, I had shared a large part of God's story—from my life and from the Bible. He said he didn't have a Bible, so I gave him mine. And that morning, as I traveled back to Plymouth, I was amazed that God had used my delay for His good.

I could also tell you about a citywide celebration I attended in an old Anglican church. I was there with Baptists, Methodists, Brethren, and Anglicans, singing praise to God. While we sang,

I felt overwhelmed by the presence of God. Then, suddenly, a beautiful picture came to mind of Jesus riding through the sky on a mighty white horse. I was behind Him, and He was showing me how dark the nations had become. However, as we passed over each bleak land, brilliant rays of light would shoot up out of the darkness. These were the faithful in times of trial. And in that moment I knew God was calling me to leave England and travel the world for His sake.

ALWAYS AMAZED

But mostly, when I think of standing amazed, I think about my mum. Of course, she isn't perfect, but for most of my life she has lived with a singular focus on God. She left school at sixteen, and she has often felt inadequate because of this, but since she became a Christian in her twenties, her vibrancy for God has never wavered.

Her prayer life amazes me. She prays for everything—from a parking space at the mall to global tragedies. I have seen her gush with awe atop a mountain in Yellowstone Park, giving glory to God. I have seen her turn to prayer immediately when she reports the misfortune of a friend. When a prayer is answered—which they often are—she broadcasts her amazement at God's provision. Not like a child who had low expectations of her parents and then received a coveted rag doll under the Christmas tree. Rather, my mum lives with a constant awareness of the majesty and transcendence of her heavenly Father, and she is never disappointed with what she receives from Him. If she has hardship, she regularly recounts how such hardship is working for good. If she sees an act of kindness, she'll whisper under her breath, "Isn't the Lord good." My mother is a book that I have read year after year and, quite frankly, have taken for granted.

My mum and my dad lived in each other's pockets since they were seventeen, but while my mother responded to God's call, my father stubbornly resisted. For over thirty years, he cut off any conversation about God. For thirty years, Mum faithfully prayed for him and lived out the presence of God in front of him and waited for God to do His good work.

Then, when Dad was just fifty-six, he was diagnosed with terminal cancer. After the doctor gave him the news, he walked Mum down to the hospital chapel and said to her, "You're going to have to help me do this." He knew he didn't have what she had, and he knew he needed it.

He agreed to do a Bible study with Mum. Through His Word, God spoke. Eventually, when Dad's pain was unbearable, he asked Mum, "If I give my life to God, will He take away the pain?" As much as she longed for Dad to be saved, she told him the truth—that no one makes a deal with God, that we must come to Him in complete surrender.

We were all in Paris—Mum and Dad, Kelli and me. Dad wanted to see the city—his favorite—for one last time. One evening Kelli and I returned to our hotel to find Mum bursting with the news. My father had given his life to God. You could have knocked me over with a feather. I had ceased to pray for his conversion and had instead spent years praying for his health and happiness. But now when health and happiness seemed to be slipping away, God had given us something far greater. He had given us more of Himself.

In the final few months of my father's life, I was even more amazed at the changes God wrought in him. My unsentimental dad threw his arms around his sister and treated her with more tenderness than I had ever seen. He joked with my uncle about their motorbikes. "You won't see me in heaven," Dad said. Then as we all exchanged concerned looks, he added the memorable punch line, "I'll be too fast."

I was most amazed one evening when he struggled down to the sofa in the living room. Mum and Kelli and I gathered around. He was not given to speeches or genuine displays of emotion or af-

> AS GOD LEADS US ON INTO A DEEPER ENCOUNTER WITH HIM, THEN WE HAVE MORE OF LIFE THAN WE COULD IMAGINE.

fection, but that night he spoke from his heart. He explained that he saw this death from pancreatic cancer as a blessing. "Some people die suddenly," he explained. "But I had a year during which I could make things right with Mum and you, Pete. And I wish I had more time to know Kelli." Then he painfully pushed himself up off the couch and made his way back upstairs to bed.

To think that a man—who had doggedly resisted his Maker for decades—would now be grateful for God's pursuit even unto death! I was confounded. My mother was not. She was grateful beyond measure, but not surprised. She had shown my father what a faithful life consumed by God could be. My faith was too small.

God is truly in the business of blowing our minds. My recognition of this has been intermittent. My eyes continue to be opened to who He is and what I truly desire. I desire Him. I was made for Him. All other relationships and all other experiences fall short in some way. But as God leads us on into a deeper encounter with Him, then we have more of life than we could imagine. Then we recognize that His artistry is reflected in the pattern on each ladybug's back that crawls in our kitchen. His majesty spreads across the flat horizons of the American Midwest and the expansive sky above. His love is laid bare each time a new life comes into this lost world. His redemption is on display each day through His faithful servants who turn the world right side up.

We don't now have minds that are capable of comprehending or bodies that are able to endure the presence of God as He really is, in all His glory. However, one day we will step out of this world and all that blinds us, and we will see Him as He is.

> *Then Joshua said to the people,*
> *"Consecrate yourselves, for tomorrow the*
> *LORD will do wonders among you."*
> —JOSHUA 3:5

ACTIONS TO CONSIDER

Write the words "Prepare to Be Amazed" on a series of 3x5 cards. Put one on your mirror, one on your dashboard, one over your kitchen sink. Place them anywhere you want to be reminded of God's amazing power and goodness.

For one day either record in a journal or verbally tell a person you're with *all* the details of God's provision and His handiwork throughout the day. How does keeping your eyes open for this change how you live?

QUESTIONS FOR REFLECTION AND DISCUSSION

- How do we push through from a spirit of entitlement to a spirit of being amazed?

- How has your experience in education, church, family, and work stripped you of your childlike sense of amazement?
- What biographies have you read of people whom God used greatly? How do their lives amaze you?
- What examples do you have from your own life of how God amazes you?
- Like Peter with his unbelieving father, what amazing thing could you be praying for and expecting from God?

OTHER THINGS TO READ

The biography of any of the following: Amy Carmichael, Jim or Elisabeth Elliot, George Mueller, Gladys Aylward, Nate Saint, or another missionary.

Matt Appling, *Life after Art: What You Forgot about Life and Faith Since You Left the Art Room* (Moody).

Joël Malm, *Vision Map: Charting a Step-by-Step Course for Your Biggest Hopes and Dreams* (Moody).

Jonathan Malm, *Created for More: 30 Days to Seeing Your World in a New Way* (Moody).

Cornelius Plantinga, *Engaging God's World: A Christian Vision of Faith, Learning, and Living* (Eerdmans).

AFTERWORD
A FEW MORE
THINGS

"Never get another perm" was Point 19 in the original "20 Things" article. I (Kelli) included it for a little bit of levity, and if you saw the picture of my twentysomething self that accompanied the post, Point 19 would need no further explanation. My mop is huge enough without any help. But wow, you should see what a little permanent wave can do!

Anyhow, in the process of writing this book, we were curious what advice our friends might give their twentysomething selves. So we surveyed a number of them. We asked a number of our favorite people: "What is one thing YOU would have told your twentysomething self? Or if you are a twentysomething, what is one thing that you have learned in life thus far?"

Here's what they had to say:

It's fine to be anxious from time to time. The world is a broken place and you should feel a little uneasy every once in a while. —MELISSA

How people treat you is more a reflection of them, not you.
—AUDREY

Appreciate and spend time with your friends. Travel. Enjoy being single. Refuse to spend too much time and worry on finding a spouse. —JAMIE

Read books by people who have been dead for a while. —KEN

You'll never understand everything in your life. In fact, it will probably feel as if you understand less and less. That's okay.
—ANDY

Accept the consequences of your behavior. Don't blame others for your own mistakes. —CAROL

Don't make life decisions based on what others want for you.
—IAN

Shoulder pads are not cool! —KIMBERLY

It's okay not to be good at everything. One day it won't matter that you can't bake a cupcake to save your life. —CATHY

People grow up and move on—family, friends, and work. You are in a constantly shifting and changing environment. Learn to invest in the moment because it won't last forever.
—TIM

The promises you made yourself as a middle- or high-schooler about how you would change the world, whom you'd marry, and how you'd look are probably all going to be broken. You won't mind. You'll make new promises and you'll set new goals. And you'll care about yourself and relationships and the world in a new way. You'll still want to change the world. You will at 30 as well. Keep goal setting and changing your part of the world. —RESA

Be gracious. Each of us is only two steps away from making a stupid decision. —LUCIE

Temporary problems may not require permanent solutions. The solutions we assume will be permanent may not be. —JENNIFER

If you don't know why you are going to college and are just there for the experience, quit. Get a real job and figure out what you like to do. —NICHOLAS

Once you get that first real job, it's probably a good idea to start a nest egg, even if you haven't found your mate yet. —JENNA

Let go of who you want to be and fall in love with who God made you to be. Once you do that, then letting your identity be in Christ is so much easier. —CRIS

Don't sweat the small stuff. Start every morning reminding yourself of the gift each new day really is. —DELIA

When certain cleaning products are mixed together, they create a hazardous chemical reaction. Do not test this concept.
—KELLI

Not everybody's rich. It's totally cool to have knockoffs. Besides, it's just a fad and will disappear in a year or two anyway. —HANNAH

Fear is one of love's greatest enemies. It can derail the love that we have for each other and prevent us from accepting the love that comes from God. Courage is a necessary component of love. —RYAN

Keep deodorant and toothpaste in your purse or bag. This applies to men too. —SARAH

That bad feeling a person or situation is giving you is your instincts doing their awesome job; you are not crazy. Speak up and establish boundaries. —LYNNAE

Don't worry about finding the "right path," the one you believe is the only way to please God. Choose something you love, are gifted in, and go for it! As long as you bring honor and glory to God through it, He will be pleased. —SHILOH

If the mainstream is pushing it, don't fall for it. Question it.
—FRED

Your life up until your 20s is all about learning. Then you enter your 20s, and it becomes so much about untangling all that you've learned. But be encouraged: unlearning is learning nonetheless—and it's the most courageous learning you'll do. —SARAH

People tell you what they really believe by their actions, not their words. Know your friends by their actions toward you. —CAMILLE

Strive to be very good at what you do, but don't get caught up in chasing perfection. —PETER

Accept your parents and how human they are. You will be like them one day. Or if you don't want to be—get thinking and praying about how to be different. —LUCIE

If you want it, but you don't need it, you don't actually want it. —MYRTLE

Do not be afraid to fail. You will miss out on so many things if you allow fear of failure to control your decisions. —GLORIA

If you're a man, let yourself cry. (But be prepared to be dumped by your girlfriend.) —PETER

Never hold on to your plans too tightly. —CARA

Take full advantage of your flexibility and freedom.
—JILL

You may be pushed so much closer to God by seeing something that He wants done and doing it—even if you feel unqualified. —SETH

Seek out mentors who can help you process your past, and others who can help you hear your future. —DUANE

There are some things you never become too old for, e.g., bubbles, coloring books, and Halloween candy. —JENNA

Do whatever you can to visit and serve the poor in a developing country. —REX

Take a second. Think things through. Engage appropriately.
—JONATHAN

NOTES

Preface

1. Alexandra Robbins and Abby Wilner, *Quarterlife Crisis: The Unique Challenges of Life in Your Twenties* (New York: Putnam, 2001), 9.
2. Alexander Maclaren, "A Young Man's Choice of Wisdom," *Bible Hub* (n.d.), http://biblehub.com/sermons/auth/maclaren/a_young_man%27s_wise_choice_op_wisdom.htm.

#1: Examine your foundation carefully

1. Christian Smith and Melinda Lundquist Denton, *Soul Searching: The Religious and Spiritual Lives of American Teenagers* (New York: Oxford University Press, 2005).

#2: Remain teachable

1. The original source of this quote is debatable and impossible to trace.
2. Paul D. Stanley and J. Robert Clinton, *Connecting: The Mentoring Relationships You Need to Succeed in Life* (Colorado Springs: NavPress, 1992), 43.

#3: Dig deeper than your doubt

1. J. P. Moreland and Klaus Issler, *In Search of a Confident Faith: Overcoming Barriers to Trusting God* (Downers Grove, IL: IVP Books, 2008), 48.
2. Carson Nyquist and Paul Nyquist, *The Post-Church Christian: Dealing with the Generational Baggage of Our Faith* (Chicago: Moody, 2013), 40.
3. Ibid.
4. Sean McDowell, "When Kids Question Their Faith," 2011, http://www.seanmcdowell.org/index.php/youth-culture/when-kids-question-their-faith/.
5. Timothy Keller, *The Reason for God: Belief in an Age of Skepticism* (New York: Dutton, 2008), 16, as quoted in Nyquist and Nyquist.
6. Nyquist and Nyquist, 41.
7. McDowell, "When Kids Question Their Faith."

#4: Choose your community carefully

1. Sherry Turkle, *Alone Together: Why We Expect More from Technology and Less from Each Other* (New York: Basic Books, 2011).
2. Ibid., 13.
3. James C. Wilhoit and John M. Dettoni, *Nurture That Is Christian: Developmental Perspectives on Christian Education* (Grand Rapids: Baker Books, 1995), 98.

4. James Fowler, *Stages of Faith: The Psychology of Human Development and the Quest for Meaning* (New York: HarperCollins, 1981), 33.

5. Alan Hirsch, *The Forgotten Ways: Reactivating the Missional Church* (Grand Rapids: Brazos Press, 2006), 219.

6. Ibid., 220–21.

#5: Feed yourself

1. Spurlock retells this narrative in the Foreword of Alex Jamieson's book *The Great American Detox Diet: 8 Weeks to Weight Loss and Well-Being* (New York: Rodale, 2005), vii–ix.

2. Cynthia L. Ogden, PhD; Margaret D. Carroll, MSPH; Brian K. Kit, MD, MPH; Katherine M. Flegal, PhD, "Prevalence of Childhood and Adult Obesity in the United States, 2011–2012," *Journal of the American Medical Association* (26 February 2014: Vol. 311, Num. 8): 806–14.

3. The Renfrew Center Foundation for Eating Disorders, "Eating Disorders 101 Guide: A Summary of Issues, Statistics and Resources," 2003.

4. Ibid.

5. Dianne Neumark-Sztainer, *"I'm, Like, SO Fat!" Helping Your Teen Make Healthy Choices about Eating and Exercise in a Weight-Obsessed World* (New York: The Guilford Press, 2005), 5.

6. Patrick F. Sullivan, "Mortality in Anorexia Nervosa," *American Journal of Psychiatry* (July 1995: Vol. 152, Issue 7): 1073–74.

7. The Renfrew Center Foundation for Eating Disorders, "Eating Disorders 101 Guide: A Summary of Issues, Statistics and Resources," 2003.

8. Nicholas Carr, "Is Google Making Us Stupid? What the Internet Is Doing to Our Brains," *Atlantic* (July/August 2008): online.

9. J. P. Moreland, *Love the Lord Your God with All Your Mind: The Role of Reason in the Life of the Soul* (Colorado Springs: NavPress, 2012).

#6: Foster good habits

1. Charles Duhigg, *The Power of Habits: Why We Do What We Do in Life and Business* (New York: Random House, 2012), xvi.

2. Ibid., 19.

3. Ibid.

4. Ibid.

5. Ibid.

6. Ibid.

7. Ibid.

8. Ibid., 33.

9. Ibid., 85.

10. Ibid., 89.

11. Ibid., 20.

#8: Be patient

1. "Ramesh Sitaraman's research shows how poor online video quality impacts

viewers," UMassCS School of Computer Science (February 4, 2013), https://www.cs.umass.edu/news/latest-news/research-online-videos.
2. Frank May and Ashwani Monga, "When Time Has a Will of Its Own, the Powerless Don't Have the Will to Wait: Anthropomorphism of Time Can Decrease Patience," *Journal of Consumer Research* (February 2014).
3. Ibid.
4. Paul Roberts, "Instant Gratification," *American Scholar* (September 8, 2014): online.
5. Ibid.
6. Jerome Daley, *When God Waits: Make Sense of Divine Delays* (Colorado Springs: WaterBrook Press, 2005), 1.7. Ibid., 10.

#9: Don't worry

1. Alisha Coleman-Jensen, Mark Nord, Margaret Andrews, and Steven Carlson, "Household Food Security in the United States in 2011," *Economic Research Report No. EER-141* (September 2012).

#10: Adjust your expectations

1. Henry Cloud, *Changes That Heal: How to Understand Your Past to Ensure a Healthier Future* (Grand Rapids: Zondervan, 2003), 170.
2. A. A. Milne, *Winnie the Pooh* (New York: Puffin Books, 1954), 70.

#11: Take risks

1. Tony Campolo, "If I Had to Live It Over Again," tonycampolo.org.

#13: Press into pain

1. C. S. Lewis, *The Problem of Pain* (New York: Macmillan, 1945).
2. Dr. Henry Cloud and Dr. John Townsend, *How People Grow: What the Bible Reveals about Personal Growth* (Grand Rapids: Zondervan, 2001), 207.
3 Ibid., 228.
4. George Barna, *Maximum Faith: Live Like Jesus* (Austin, TX: Fedd and Company, 2011), 22.
5 Ibid.
6. Ibid.
7. Robert Sears, "Model for Spiritual Development." Handout, n.d.
8. "About Ed's Story," Flannel (2015), edsstory.com.
9. Charles Dickens, *A Tale of Two Cities* (New York: Barnes and Noble Books, 2004).

#15: Embrace grace

1. Victor Hugo, *Les Miserables* (New York: Signet Classics, 1987).

#16: Seek healing

1. Karl Lehman, *Outsmarting Yourself: Catching Your Past Invading the Present and What to Do about It* (Libertyville, IL: This Joy! Books, 2011), 13.

2. Ibid., 16.

3. Ibid., 13.

#17: Live loved

1. *The Last of the Mohicans,* Dir. Michael Mann, Perf. Daniel Day-Lewis, Fox Home Entertainment, 1992.

2. C. S. Lewis, *The Four Loves* (Orlando: Harcourt, 1960).

3. Gary Chapman, *The 5 Love Languages: The Secret to Love That Lasts* (Chicago: Northfield Publishing, 1992, 2015).

ACKNOWLEDGMENTS

Our humble thanks . . .

To our pastors and friends at the following churches, who have fed us and loved us and provided us with a spiritual home: Underwood Chapel, Southview Baptist, Faith Baptist, Fox Valley Bible, Hi Praz Bible Fellowship, Rogers Park Community Church, Grace Fellowship, and The Chapel.

To the many wonderful people at the following organizations, who have given us the opportunity to discuss and hone the ideas found in this book: Lake Geneva Youth Camp and Conference Center, Trinity Evangelical Divinity School, Moody Bible Institute, and The Covenant, Cornerstone, and Crossroads groups from The Moody Church.

To our agent, Austin Wilson, and our editors at Moody Publishers for believing in this project and making it happen.

To all of the twentysomethings who have shared their lives with us over a cup of tea and a piece of caramel shortbread.

To our friends and family who have supported us and encouraged us and prayed for us along the way. Especially to Mum, who keeps our family afloat in so many necessary ways.

Most of all, to our Lord Jesus Christ, the author and perfecter of our faith.

ABOUT THE AUTHORS

Peter is an associate professor of education and Kelli is a professor of communications at Moody Bible Institute in Chicago. Kelli has a master of religious education degree from Trinity Evangelical Divinity School (TEDS) and a master of fine arts degree in creative writing from Roosevelt University. Peter has a master of arts degree in biblical studies from Moody Graduate School and a master of arts degree in teaching from National Louis University. He is currently pursuing a PhD in educational studies at TEDS.

Peter and Kelli speak at churches, retreats, camps, and conferences. Kelli also writes at www.thisoddhouse.org. They have developed a Bible study to accompany each chapter of this book. You can download these studies for FREE at their website (PeterandKelli.org).

Peter and Kelli live in McHenry, Illinois, with their two children, Daryl and Amelia.

Other Moody Collective Books

Join our email newsletter list to get resources and encouragement as you build a deeper faith.

Moody Collective brings words of life to a generation seeking deeper faith. We are a part of Moody Publishers, representing this next generation of followers of Christ through books on creativity, travel, the gospel, storytelling, decision making, leadership, and more.

We seek to know, love, and serve the millennial generation with grace and humility. Each of our books is intended to challenge and encourage our readers as they pursue God.

When you sign up for our newsletter, you'll get our emails twice a month. These will include the best of the resources we've seen online, book deals and giveaways, plus behind-the-scenes and extra content from our books and authors. Sign up at *www.moodycollective.com.*

a part of Moody Publishers

HOW DO YOU PACK FOR ALL FIFTY STATES?

When I was in college, I figured my life would come together around graduation. I'd meet a guy; we'd plan a beautiful wedding and buy a nice house—not necessarily with a picket fence, but with whatever kind of fence we wanted. I might work, or I might not, but whatever we decided, I would be happy.

When I got out of college and my life didn't look like that, I floundered around, trying to figure out how to get the life I had always dreamed of. Just when I had given up all hope of finding the "life I'd always dreamed about," I decided to take a trip to all fifty states...because when you go on a trip, you can't take your baggage. What I found was that "packing light" wasn't as easy as I thought it was.

This is the story of that trip and learning to live life with less baggage.
also available as an ebook

MOODY Publishers™

From the Word to Life

www.MoodyPublishers.com